Alcohemy

"Why", "Belief" and "How" are the focus points in David's Alcohemy. He shows how the mind is our greatest asset in changing any negative habitual behavior. David went from the very depths of alcohol dependency to blissfully alcohol-free by changing how he thought about alcohol use. Since 1934 Alcoholics Anonymous has earned a tremendous reputation world-wide for helping millions of people with addictions. Seventy-five years from now, David's book Alcohemy will have done the same.

—**Bob Proctor**, best-selling author, *You Were Born Rich*

This amazing book will truly help you see what is possible and live a richer life at the next level!" "When I work with my life and business planning clients, I challenge them to think differently about what is and what is possible. Then, we create the plan of action needed to get to what is possible. *Alcohemy* is a powerful life plan for people struggling with alcohol dependency, or any other negative habit. It's clear throughout the book that David Norman is committed to helping people deal with these challenges successfully.

—**Linda McLean**, Speaker, Coach and #1 International Bestselling Author of *Next Level Living: Today's Guide for Tomorrow's Abundant Life.*

David's *Alcohemy* not only reveals the real and hidden consequences of alcohol dependency, also the step-by-step process to being alcohol-free. He himself rose from the darkness and struggle to be completely free from desiring alcohol at all; simply by changing the way he thought. This should be a compelling read for all that habitually use alcohol.

—**Bill Harris**, Director, Centerpointe Research Institute, Inc., Creators of The Holosync Solution and The Life Principles Integration Process

"Powerful, life-changing! David's open, honest approach to life, love and the road to recovery are riveting. His step-by-step process encourages and empowers the individual to take charge of their own lives, reminding them that the power to choose their own destiny is already inside them. His discreet, dignified, do-it-yourself solution is a powerful remedy for any dependency or addiction and simultaneously provides the reader confidence to repair and heal the past. Alcohemy is a true catalyst for change! David delivers his disciples from the depths of alcohol dependency, to leading a life filled with their greatest dreams and desires! Cheers to your success David!"

—**Michelle Corr,** Host of Michelle Corr 6° on Voice America & KWSS 93.9 FM & CEO of 6° Media

David's journey through life and personal transformation has proven once again that nothing is more powerful than the mind. After years of struggle and heartache, David tapped deep into his own mind and developed his innate abilities to utilize this most powerful tool. However, he didn't just stop once he broke through; he continually backed his efforts with positive influences and named his process Alcohemy. He now shares the secret of his personal success in the hope that others can experience the joy of living a life free from negative habitual behaviour. This is a must read for anyone concerned about creating sustained change in their life.

—**Michael Fitzgerald, Sr.** Co-Founder of MyCause Water

Alcohemy is a refreshing look into the how and why behind addiction, and David Norman's story gives powerful insight into the role of the mind, emotion and belief in finding healing.

—**Dina Proctor**, Best-Selling Author of *Madly Chasing Peace*

As a scientist by training, I was rather skeptical when I realized that this book is basically a personal story. A case of one can be misleading. All of us are unique and different, and what works for David may well only work for him. What convinces me is experimental evidence, controls and comparisons.

However, as I read on, I became more and more impressed. Either David is a genius who invented all this, or he has trained himself very well indeed in the fine details of psychotherapy. I have worked as a counseling psychologist since 1991, and a great deal of the contents of this book could have come from my case notes with clients. I have not found a single statement in *Alcohemy* that is not evidence-based.

The method described in this book worked for David, and will work for you, because it is best psychotherapeutic practice.

At the same time, it is new and novel. Like everyone else, until I read *Alcohemy*, I believed that an alcoholic can only become a dry alcoholic, because the condition is a disease, as stated by AA. I agreed with the general assessment that many years of abstinence can be broken if an alcoholic takes a drink, even unknowingly. The urge, the desire is always there in the background.

David has convinced me that it is possible to get rid of this urge, this desire to drink alcohol, and by implication to get rid of any other addiction. I have started to apply David's ideas in my therapeutic practice, and hope the book will be widely enough known that it becomes the new accepted wisdom.

—**Dr Bob Rich**, MSc, PhD, MAPS, Counselling Psychologist
Member of the Australian Psychological Society
Member, APS College of Counselling Psychologists
Member, International Positive Psychology Association

Alcohemy

The Solution to Ending
Your Alcohol Habit for Good

Privately, Discreetly, and
Fully in Control

David Norman

New York

ALCOHEMY
The Solution to Ending Your Alcohol Habit for Good—
Privately, Discreetly, and Fully in Control

© 2014 David Norman. All rights reserved.

All rights reserved. No portion of this book may be reproduced, stored in a retrieval system, or transmitted in any form or by any means—electronic, mechanical, photocopy, recording, scanning, or other,—except for brief quotations in critical reviews or articles, without the prior written permission of the publisher.

Published in New York, New York, by Morgan James Publishing. Morgan James and The Entrepreneurial Publisher are trademarks of Morgan James, LLC.
www.MorganJamesPublishing.com

The Morgan James Speakers Group can bring authors to your live event. For more information or to book an event visit The Morgan James Speakers Group at www.TheMorganJamesSpeakersGroup.com.

ISBN 978-1-61448-571-1 paperback
ISBN 978-1-61448-868-2 hard cover
ISBN 978-1-61448-572-8 eBook
ISBN 978-1-61448-573-5 audio
Library of Congress Control Number: 2013940381

Cover Design by:
Rachel Lopez
www.r2cdesign.com

Interior Design by:
Bonnie Bushman
bonnie@caboodlegraphics.com

In an effort to support local communities, raise awareness and funds, Morgan James Publishing donates a percentage of all book sales for the life of each book to Habitat for Humanity Peninsula and Greater Williamsburg.

Get involved today, visit
www.MorganJamesBuilds.com.

Medical Disclaimer

(1) No advice

This book has been written as an information resource to help increase awareness of alcohol dependency. It contains general information about alcohol consumption, effects and possible treatment options. The information is not professional or medical advice, and should not be treated as such.

(2) No warranties

Any medical information in this book is provided without any representations or warranties, express or implied. The author makes no representations or warranties in relation to the information in this book.

Without prejudice to the generality of the foregoing paragraph, we do not warrant that:

- (a) the medical information in this book will be constantly available, or available at all; or
- (b) the medical information in this book is complete, true, accurate, up-to-date, or non-misleading.

(3) Professional assistance

You must not rely on the information in this book as an alternative to medical advice from your doctor or other professional healthcare provider.

If you have any specific questions about any medical matter you should consult your doctor or other professional healthcare provider. If you think you may be suffering from any medical condition you should seek immediate medical attention. You should never delay seeking medical advice, disregard medical advice, or discontinue medical treatment because of information in this book.

(4)   Limiting our liability
Nothing in this medical disclaimer will:

- (a) limit or exclude our liability for death or personal injury resulting from negligence;
- (b) limit or exclude our liability for fraud or fraudulent misrepresentation;
- (c) limit any of our liabilities in any way that is not permitted under applicable law; or
- (d) exclude any of our liabilities that may not be excluded under applicable law.

Contents

Introduction ... xi

Part One: Exposing Alcohol Dependency ... 1

Chapter 1	What the Brew Will Do to You	3
Chapter 2	My Personal Struggle with Alcohol Dependency	15
Chapter 3	Searching for a Remedy	54
Chapter 4	The Remedy Revealed	81

Part Two: The Alcohemy Process ... 99

Element 1	Your Journey's History	101
Element 2	Record Your Associations with Alcohol	115
Element 3	Record Your Life Values	118
Element 4	Record What Alcohol Does for You	121
Element 5	Record the Effects of Ceasing Your Habit	130
Element 6	Record the Effects of *NOT* Ceasing Your Habit	133
Element 7	Record the Compilation of Total Effects of Consuming Alcohol versus Current Values	136
Element 8	Record and Replace the Fears That Are Holding You Back	140

Element 9	Record Your Current Actions Involving Alcohol and Replace Them with New Actions	148
Element 10	Prepare Answers to Likely Questions and Statements Regarding Your New Habit	165
Element 11	Write Your Commitment Statement	178
Element 12	Document and Reward Milestones	182
Element 13	Plan Your Start Date and *Start*	192
Conclusion	The Power of Alcohemy	197
Appendix:	The Element Workbook	203
	Acknowledgments	217
	About the Author	219

Introduction

Oh shit, it's happened again! What did I do last night? I can't remember. Jeez, I hope I didn't do or say anything to embarrass myself or Donna. It couldn't have been good though as I feel like crap this morning and once again can't remember anything past . . . what is my last clear memory? Think, man, think! I'll just lie here pretending to be asleep until I can recall enough of the night's events so I can at least have a bit of a chance of defending myself when Donna wakes up. Bloody hell, I hate it when I drink too much and can't remember what's happened. I can't keep doing this to myself or her. But what the hell do I do? I don't believe I could ever stop drinking completely.

This thought process was typical of what used to go through my mind all too frequently on weekend mornings for many years. It was even more of a common occurrence when I was younger and unmarried and partied harder and more frequently. Actually, in those days I didn't need a party; I often just drank with or without company, weekdays or weekends—it didn't matter.

You could say I was living an ordinary life, living in the seaside city of Hervey Bay in Queensland, Australia, married with two sons, and working as a staff supervisor for an electricity distribution company. My general circumstances would be similar to those of hundreds of millions of people around the world, particularly given that more than 3.5 billion adults globally drink alcohol. Unfortunately I also became a less desirable World Health Organization (WHO) statistic as one of 140 million who developed an alcohol dependency and one of more than 400 million with alcohol-related problems. According to a WHO document, 78 percent of people don't seek help and their dependency goes untreated. Furthermore, 2.5 million people die annually from harmful use of alcohol. Sadly, of these approximately 320,000 are young people between fifteen and twenty.[1]

Drinking is what Aussies do—I simply couldn't imagine life without alcohol. My social life depended on it, my ability to relax and unwind depended on it, and my ability to feel good at all depended on it. In other words, *I* depended on it. And so did most people around me. I prided myself on being a clear and analytical thinker and completely devoted to my family. Yet week after week my alcohol habit would lead me to act in ways completely incongruous with my personality and my values, and ultimately threatened all I held dear. I felt powerless to change.

However, even though I was beginning to admit that I had a deep-seated dependency on alcohol, I did not see myself as what I pictured to be a typical alcoholic. To me the word "alcoholic" conjured up visions of someone living on the streets or in homeless shelters, with ragged clothes and drinking out of a bottle in a paper bag—or at best someone who couldn't hold down or function properly in their job, was sneaking alcohol at every chance available, and had abusive relationships with family and friends (if any at all). Even though I obviously had alcohol-related problems, my internal sense of dignity and self-esteem and a deep knowing of who I really was without the impact of alcohol prevented me from using those forms of assistance. I flatly refused to consider going to a support group like Alcoholics Anonymous (AA) or even discussing it with my regular doctor. Even though I knew I had a very serious habit that was resulting in embarrassing behavior, my tenacious pride and core belief that

---

[1] World Health Organization, *Global Status Report on Alcohol and Health* (WHO Press, 2011), http://www.who.int/substance_abuse/publications/global_alcohol_report/msbgsruprofiles.pdf.
World Health Organization, *Mental Health Around the World – Stop Exclusion Dare to Care*, http://www.who.int/world-health-day/previous/2001/files/whd2001_dare_to_care_en.pdf
World Health Organization, *Management of Substance Abuse – Facts and Figures*, http://www.who.int/substance_abuse/facts/en/

I was an intelligent and very good person at heart (not a "typical" alcoholic) prohibited me from seeking support-group assistance.

I want to be clear: I have nothing against organizations like Alcoholics Anonymous. I believe they form an important support network for people with alcohol problems who don't have the tools, knowledge, or motivation to manage on their own. Personally, though, there was no way in a pink fit that I was going to submit myself to the humiliation of publically declaring I was a hopeless drunk or had lost full control of any part of my life. Such was my obstinate mindset: I was going to do it myself, or not at all.

This resolve was the main driving force that eventually led me to develop a private DIY method (that I could work through *by myself*) that released me from the habit and bonds of alcohol dependency forever. After several years of reading and listening to personal growth material, I started to see there may be a way to give my habit a good shake and possibly break free. It began with discovering the power of belief. I had the profound realization that anything was possible with belief—and nothing was possible without it. But I also knew the standard wisdom on alcohol dependency: once an alcoholic, always an alcoholic. Could the power of belief be applied to my alcohol habit?

When I finally believed I could be alcohol-free, the process of how began to reveal itself to me, piece by piece. After even more research and many months of quality time analyzing what it would take to develop a non-drinker's mindset, I slowly devised and worked through a series of mental exercises and elements that I believed would be necessary for permanent change.

What I ended up creating for myself was a fully comprehensive plan from start to finish that covers all the aspects I had to think about, prepare for, and deal with in order to become truly alcohol-free. Much to my absolute elation, this process did what I expected it would. I have been free from *even the thought of* needing alcohol ever since. Drinking alcohol literally does not enter into my consciousness as an option, and, as I prefer to phrase it now, "alcohol is irrelevant to my desires."

Although I didn't realize it at the time, the process I discovered is the same basic process that lies behind establishing any new habit, whether large or small—as recent behavioral studies have shown. It all comes down to the *why*, *belief*, and *how* behind your behavior. First you must understand *why* you engage in your current unwanted behaviors and what benefits they bring you, as well as why you want to establish new, better behaviors. Second, you must *believe* that it is possible for you to change. And third, you must lay out exactly *how* you are going to make this change in your behavior, step by step.

You can successfully apply this general process to any habitual behavior you'd like to change (I have since changed many old habits using this process), but what I think is revolutionary about this book is that I've discovered you can successfully apply it to alcohol dependency as well—which current cultural (and even psychological and medical) wisdom says is a lifelong condition and is impossible to fully eradicate. My experience has proven that this just isn't the case.

I am fully aware that this position directly contradicts the wisdom behind a program that has been a respected part of our culture for more than one hundred years. But I am convinced that my do-it-yourself self-help program can reach so many more people struggling with alcohol habits who would naturally resist going to their doctor or public forums for help.

The Alcohemy process is a way to free yourself from the bonds of your alcohol habit quietly and privately through a process that puts the power back into your hands and allows you to retain your personal dignity, self-respect, and privacy. You remain in control, and you choose *if* you tell others, when you tell others, whom you tell, and how much you tell them. The long-term benefits of being in control of the entire process—from the journey of understanding why you started your alcohol habit, to identifying your beliefs about drinking versus ceasing, to analyzing your fears and choosing the reasons you want to stop—all make this *your* process. This gives you and you alone the power over your destiny. I believe this is far more powerful and results in a far greater chance of lifelong results than having a support group or private practitioner tell you what to think and do, and then hold your hand all the way through.

The risk with that approach is when the outside support is no longer there, you have a reduced inner substance or self-belief to fall back on. If it felt to you that someone else was really driving your success, and you were just following orders, when they are gone, what then? If you perceived they had the power to make sure you achieved your results, not you, you will most likely need their ongoing support for life, for fear of relapsing back into your old ways. You would have to ask yourself, "Where did the true power to change come from: you, or the support person or group?"

My process, on the other hand, was a completely self-driven journey of discovery, personalized according to where I came from and why I had an alcohol habit. All my analysis was spent digging into my own experiences, thoughts, and feelings about alcohol in my life. Every element of the process was about my personal beliefs, fears, and hopes. I had to make choices and decisions about my own responses to my family and my friends. How I prepared to handle different situations was up to me: I chose my start date, my milestones, and how I rewarded myself. Ultimately I took responsibility for the detail and the execution of my plan, and, yes, I damned well am taking credit for my fantastic success!

Most significantly, following the process, my support system didn't ride off into the sunset and leave me alone floundering into the future. The sense of self-achievement I got from what I accomplished on my own is incredible and has since led to other successful feats and opened up further possibilities in other areas of my life. Because I did it myself, the belief, confidence, and power remain with me forever.

By changing from the inside out rather than trying to control behaviors from the outside in (through the combination of the why, the how, and belief process I will explain in detail throughout the book), I have truly been alcohol-free since then. The self-directed process made me not just free of alcohol, but free *from* alcohol. The result was an utter transformation: even though my body and external appearance were the same, my spirit had been completely transformed in a profound and positive way.

Because this transformation went so far beyond the mere outward action of consuming alcohol, I refer to my process as *Alcohemy*. "Alchemy" has been defined as a "magical power or process of transmuting a common substance (usually of little value), into a substance of great value." It was practiced mainly in the Middle Ages to try to turn base metals into gold and to discover an "elixir of life," resulting in great power to the person who could succeed.

We may never know whether anyone actually found the elixir of life or turned lead into gold with alchemy, but I have proof that my Alcohemy can indeed turn wine into water. Before the end of my alcohol habit, red wine was my drink of choice and I consumed it every single day. Now, apart from the occasional apple juice, just about the only thing I ever drink is water. Yes, plain, as unadulterated as possible, natural, healthy water. I know that many people who regularly drink alcohol, soft drinks, coffee, tea, juices, and other artificially flavored beverages will have a very hard time comprehending that I enjoy and now prefer pure water. But the fact is that water has been the only thing that has ever really quenched my thirst. After all, that is the only real reason we need to drink: to replace and maintain our body fluids, which are all water-based.

So not only did my Alcohemy process turn wine into water, it may well have revealed that the real elixir of life was literally right under my nose all along: healthy, natural water.

But Alcohemy does much more than change wine into water. It transforms our very nature. I transformed myself from the low-value base of my alcohol dependency, characterized by constant struggle and frustration, to a valuable, highly rewarded husband, father, friend, colleague, and member of the world community. I turned an ordinary existence into one that has new, expanded goals and expectations of achievement, power, passion, and promise, and I turned my lifelong desire to make a difference into the reality of touching and helping the lives of many people around the world. The changes and rewards I have experienced after leaving my alcohol-fueled life behind and embracing my alcohol-free lifestyle have truly been priceless.

I did my apprenticeship the hard way: over years of personal frustration, heartache, and trial and error. But with determination and the belief that I could be the master of my fate, I slowly uncovered the secret elements to my complete transformation. Although the ancient art of alchemy may have been practiced by conjuring up spells and/or blending unusual and rare ingredients, the magical power of my Alcohemy process is available to anyone who really desires it. The only difference is that if you follow the process described in this book, you will complete the transformation in a fraction of the time it took me.

This book is not about preaching to everyone that they should never drink the "demon" alcohol (even though it is the best option for your well-being). My primary reason for writing this book is to share a discreet, dignified, do-it-yourself solution with people who find themselves unhappy with their alcohol habit and the problems it causes them. The Alcohemy process is for people who desire a better quality of life and better-quality relationships, and realize that their habitual alcohol consumption inhibits that quality.

If you're wondering whether your alcohol consumption has become a habit or even a dependency, I just have one question for you. Could you easily go thirty days without having an alcoholic drink or feeling like you need to have one? If you cannot honestly answer yes, then you have some degree of alcohol dependency.

The good news is that an alcohol dependency doesn't have to be a life sentence. I don't expect that every habitual drinker will be committed to quit their habit or even believe it is possible to quit their habit at this stage, though it is important that they have the desire or an open mind about changing their current behavior. I believe that when we're born, every one of us is connected to an innate power that impels us to be the best we can. Some have a very strong bond with that energy and achieve great things, while others lose the initial connection we were born with along the way and lead ordinary lives. If you desire to change your life for the better, it is my belief that by reading this book, you will gain not only the belief and commitment to change your habit, but the practical process to succeed long term.

However, this book was not written just with heavily alcohol-dependent people in mind. It is also for new and low-to-moderate consumers of alcohol who realize their regular habit is not serving them with any real benefit. I really want to help prevent new or moderate alcohol consumers from going down the easily traveled dependency path like I did. I know only too well the pain that leads to. But even if a low-to-moderate alcohol habit never leads to any visibly negative effects, it will certainly keep you from ever achieving your full potential in your personal or business life.

In our modern-day, fast-paced, and predominantly competitive world, where it is an advantage to always be alert, in control of your senses, and on top of your game, it is a distinct disadvantage to have any alcohol habit or dependency. You will never be as successful as you truly could be if you have an alcohol habit. With an increasing awareness and focus on personal health and financial security globally, it is time that we as individuals, communities, and countries earnestly assess what role alcohol plays in our lives and its necessity. I believe the global answer will be, as I found when I went through this process, that alcohol consumption serves no positive benefit that can't be achieved by healthier options.

The Alcohemy process will provide anyone seeking to reach their full potential the required mindset and proven process to successfully achieve an alcohol-free life. Nevertheless, the most dramatic changes will be seen in those who have an established dependency that causes multiple problems for themselves, family, friends, and colleagues. It can be very demoralizing, demeaning, and life-limiting to the person with the dependency, who when unaffected by alcohol is intelligent, is good natured, and possesses great natural potential in life. This was how I felt, and I suffered in quiet desperation as I battled my inner demons, believing that because my alcohol habit had been such a long-term, firmly entrenched habit, I would have it until I died.

In that light, this book is also for family, friends, and associates of someone with an alcohol dependency, offering firsthand insight on how the person with the habit may be struggling internally. It can be such an embarrassing and personally humiliating topic that quite often they won't want to fully open up to loved ones or even admit the extent of the problem to themselves. Again, this is how I felt. Even though my perception eventually changed from "it is a normal Aussie habit to drink a fair bit" to "I have a serious dependency on alcohol that is causing me and my family far too many problems and embarrassment," I was still reluctant to fully discuss it with my wife, let alone anyone else. No matter why you are reading this book or how you came to have it, it is by no accident. I firmly believe that you were meant to have this knowledge for your own or someone else's benefit, and your commitment and sacrifice of the time it takes you to read it will be rewarded in ways you don't even realize at this time.

If you are like I was and recognize you have a detrimental alcohol habit but want to resolve it discreetly and with as much dignity as possible, you hold the solution in your hands. Alcohemy provides you an opportunity to make deep inner changes, resulting in a permanent alcohol-free, rewarded lifestyle—all accomplished with dignity and in as much privacy as you choose.

However, you will first need to set aside any status or airs and graces you may have and read this book as the "real" you, from your heart as well as your head. It doesn't matter whether you are a wealthy, high-level professional person or someone struggling to make ends meet. Everyone with an alcohol dependency is on the same playing field with the same psychological rules; money can't buy your way out of making the mental changes that only *you* can make. As I found, your ego and pride can be your worst enemies, as your perceived level of status can generate fears that prevent you from even trying to attempt the changes you will need to. The permanent solution is the same for everyone, so you will need to get your ego out of the way and be brutally honest with yourself and all your thoughts and actions from this point forward.

Also, I want to clearly state that I am neither a professional writer nor a university professor delivering some potential, unproven, theoretical solution. I am an ordinary, fair dinkum Aussie bloke who has personally experienced a very frustrating and soul-searching journey of years of alcohol dependency and who now lives an alcohol-free lifestyle. I may be an ordinary bloke, but I chose the path less traveled by the masses, which therefore produced uncommon, fulfilling results. My journey has been one of extremes, from experiencing the depths of despair and embarrassment through to the absolute elation of success and freedom.

If you have an alcohol dependency of your own, I know what you are feeling and empathize with your plight. If someone you care about has an alcohol problem, I understand how this affects you and your frustration and concern. There is only heartache and despair on both sides of the problem. For both of you I offer my personal experience and the thirteen-element method I created that resulted in my complete freedom from even the desire to drink alcohol. Yes, not just being able to resist the temptation to drink alcohol, but feeling that alcohol is irrelevant and I don't need or have the inclination to drink it. That is the true freedom I found.

Furthermore, to prove beyond a shadow of a doubt that I have been where you are, I want to talk about my own journey as openly and honestly as I can (without intruding on the privacy of others) and hope that any rawness in my story and literary skill is taken in the context of who I am: a ridgy-didge Aussie bloke who had enough of being a slave to alcohol and developed a process to break free forever.

Before we get under way, I'd like to share with you a poem titled 'Invictus' (Latin for 'unconquered') by William Ernest Henley. I first heard it on a Bob Proctor audio recording some years ago, and I would like you to keep it in mind as your own journey of perhaps initial despair, but then discovery and elation, unfolds throughout this book. It resonated strongly with me, and I believe it captures the attitude and many of the emotions I experienced through my years of struggle toward an alcohol-free lifestyle.

Invictus

Out of the night that covers me,
Black as the Pit from pole to pole,
I thank whatever gods may be
For my unconquerable soul.

In the fell clutch of circumstance
I have not winced nor cried aloud.
Under the bludgeonings of chance
My head is bloody, but unbowed.

Beyond this place of wrath and tears
Looms but the Horror of the shade,
And yet the menace of the years
Finds and shall find me unafraid.

It matters not how strait the gate,
How charged with punishments the scroll.
I am the master of my fate:
I am the captain of my soul.

PART ONE

EXPOSING ALCOHOL DEPENDENCY

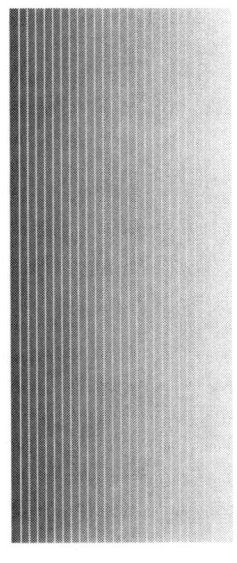

CHAPTER 1

WHAT THE BREW WILL DO TO YOU

As the statistics cited earlier show, alcohol consumption is an accepted practice in most countries worldwide. It dates back to approximately 9000 BC to simple fermented beverages and has advanced over time to include complex fermentation, brewing, distilling, and blending processes. Alcohol consumption has been used for everything from personal relaxation and social celebrations, to health remedies, trade and bartering, formal etiquette (like toasting the bride and groom), and religious ceremonies. If taken infrequently and not in excess, it should not pose a significant problem for most people. In fact, some research even suggested that a regular small amount of alcohol is good for the cardiovascular system. However, that has been disputed and even if there is some truth, it is probably where any personal benefits of alcohol consumption stops.

Unfortunately, alcohol consumption is also the cause of a huge amount of misery around the world. The negative effects of alcohol consumption are far reaching and pervade every aspect of human life, from physical and mental health to safety and finance. These consequences are not confined to the actual purchase price and health result of alcohol consumption; the incidental costs of poor judgment and decision making resulting from intoxication also need to be considered. All too often reckless choices made while under the influence of alcohol with regard to associated habits like gambling, smoking cigarettes, doing illicit drugs, as well as engaging in risky sexual activity result in a greater personal cost.

Furthermore, the price we pay for alcohol-related problems is not limited to the immediate health and financial effects on us personally; they extend to the community, state, country, and global levels. Though the toll on an individual's personal physical and mental health and finances is bad enough, collectively this equates to massive amounts of money to state and national governments worldwide in provision of health care and support services. In a recent analysis pulling together cost studies from four high-income countries and two middle-income countries, the total costs attributable to alcohol ranged from 1.3 to 3.3 percent of gross domestic product.[2] The social cost of alcohol use was approximately US$216 billion in the United States (2000) and US$5.2 billion in Australia (1998).[3]

Of course, when I was looking for a solution to my alcohol habit, I was not focused on the global or even the community repercussions. I was more concerned with my own life and how it was affecting my relationships, health, personal development, work, and finances (and in that order, by the way). Only during my further research of the subject and when I realized I could help others achieve my alcohol-free results did I understand the magnitude of the global problem. Quoting statistics might be boring to some people, but I thought the following stats gave some extra insight on not only how alcohol consumption is a problem for individuals and

---

[2] World Health Organization, *Global Status Report on Alcohol and Health* (WHO Press, 2011), http://www.who.int/substance_abuse/publications/global_alcohol_report/msbgsruprofiles.pdf.

[3] Global Health Observatory Data Repository, World Health Organization, accessed April 9, 2013, http://apps.who.int/gho/data/node.main.A1118?lang=en.

their families, but also how it is causing major issues around the world. According the World Health Organization's *Global Report on Alcohol and Health* (2011):[4]

- 2.5 million people die annually from harmful use of alcohol.
- Almost 4 percent of all deaths worldwide are attributed to alcohol, a greater number than deaths caused by HIV/AIDS, violence, or tuberculosis.
- Globally, 6.2 percent of all male deaths are attributable to alcohol, compared to 1.1 percent of female deaths. The harmful use of alcohol is especially fatal for younger age groups, and alcohol is the world's leading risk factor for death among males aged fifteen to fifty-nine.
- Heavy episodic drinking is another important pattern of drinking because it leads to serious health problems and is particularly associated with injury. Worldwide, about 11.5 percent of drinkers have heavy episodic drinking occasions, with men outnumbering women by four to one. Men consistently engage in hazardous drinking at much higher levels than women in all regions.
- High-income countries generally have the highest alcohol consumption. However, it does not follow that high income and high consumption always translate into high alcohol-related problems and high-risk drinking.
- The highest consumption levels can be found in the developed world, mostly in the Northern Hemisphere, but also in Argentina, Australia, and New Zealand. Medium consumption levels can be found in southern Africa, with Namibia and South Africa having the highest levels, and in North and South America.
- Alcohol consumption has been identified as carcinogenic for the following cancer categories: cancers of the colorectum, female breast, larynx, liver, esophagus, oral cavity, and pharynx. The higher the consumption of alcohol, the greater the risk for these

---

[4] World Health Organization, *Global Status Report on Alcohol and Health* (WHO Press, 2011), http://www.who.int/substance_abuse/publications/global_alcohol_report/msbgsruprofiles.pdf.

cancers: even the consumption of two drinks per day causes an increased risk for some cancers, such as breast cancer.
- Approximately 4.5 percent of the global burden of disease and injury is attributable to alcohol. Alcohol consumption is estimated to cause from 20 percent to 50 percent of cirrhosis of the liver, epilepsy, poisonings, road traffic accidents, violence, and several types of cancer. It is the third highest risk for disease and disability, after childhood underweight and unsafe sex.
- An intoxicated person can put people in harm's way by involving them in traffic accidents or violent behavior, or by negatively affecting co-workers, relatives, friends, or strangers. A survey in Australia found that two-thirds of respondents were adversely affected by someone else's drinking in the past year. The drinking of a stranger negatively impacted a total of 10.5 million people.
- In the WHO Global Survey on Alcohol and Health (2008), the five-year trend of drinking among 13- to 15-year-olds was assessed: out of seventy-three responding countries, 71 percent indicated an increase. The five-year trend of drinking among eighteen- to twenty-five-year-olds indicated that, out of eighty-two responding countries, 80 percent showed an increase. One reason could be the use of flavored alcoholic carbonate drinks, also known as "alcopops," that is equated with more problematic drinking patterns, such as more frequent drinking, earlier onset of alcohol consumption, drunkenness, and more alcohol-related negative consequences.

Even though most countries with medium to high economic status now have educational programs advising of the problems associated with habitual alcohol consumption, it is still widely accepted as part of our modern lifestyle. But it doesn't have to be a totally out of control drinking habit to have negative consequences on you or your family, friends, or colleagues. Even what some people consider moderate regular consumption or infrequent heavy drinking episodes can have significant impacts. Unwanted incidents such as rape, drowning, poisoning, violence, theft, vandalism, vehicle accidents, falls, and antisocial behavior like intimidation and harassment at times can all be a direct or indirect result of inappropriate heavy episodic alcohol consumption. The reality is, apart from companies associated with the commercial aspects, consuming alcohol does not positively benefit societies at large or individuals looking to achieve their greatest potential during their lives.

In fact, today, as we are advancing technologically and psychologically at an ever increasing rate, individuals need to be sharp and on top of their game no matter where their interests lie. People are looking for the edge by continually developing innovative or better ways to do things with products and services. In the employment arena, employers are seeking high performance and maximum return for wages from staff and are therefore screening for staff willing to exceed standard expectations. In this climate of rapid change, people are required learn fast and adapt quickly. Those wanting to be successful in their chosen field have to be willing to go the extra yard to provide great quality and value to their customers. This does not just apply to typical commerce; it is likewise true in modern day sports and entertainment. There is a very fine line between a good performance and a great performance. Pushing past the traditional belief and performance boundaries reaps the rewards and raises the bar for oneself and others. I have heard and read it takes a minimum of ten thousand hours of doing something to become world-class at it. To achieve that requires a passion, belief, and commitment beyond what the average person is willing to put forth. Yet the amazing thing is we all have the ability to be world-class at something if we choose to engage those three characteristics: *passion, belief, and commitment.*

No matter what your chosen field may be, whether it's business, sports, or entertainment, there is one thing I am certain of. It is highly unlikely that anyone will achieve their full potential in the modern era if they have an alcohol habit. Even in the music industry, the expectations for greater value require soloists and music groups to perform at their peak, which would unlikely be sustained if individuals are dependent on alcohol. A significant number of groups and soloists now perform more like athletes, combining singing, playing, dancing, acting, and engaging the audience with stories or comedy. To be at your best and deliver a world-class performance, you have to be very fit, energetic, and sharp-minded. Regular alcohol consumption or heavy episodic drinking is not beneficial to achieving those qualities.

There have been many highly publicized occurrences of celebrities' careers crashing and burning because of problems with alcohol abuse. I believe, even more so now in this day and age, that high-profile business, sports, and entertainment personalities are expected to conduct themselves as good role models for the next generation of young people, inspiring them to excel in their field. Leaving these younger impressionable minds with a clear message that success can be earned and enjoyed by choosing to live with passion, belief, commitment, and a healthy lifestyle could be one of their greatest services provided and legacies left.

Apart from the high business and career expectations in today's current climate, alcohol has negative implications for modern personal and community relationships as well. People used to fall in love and marry with ironclad vows of "honor and obey, for richer or poorer, in sickness and in health, until death do us part." It was expected that the couple would make the marriage work regardless of what the actual relationship between them was like. If the relationship wasn't providing the partners with what they individually desired, they were expected to quietly put up with their dissatisfaction and settle for and adapt to their discontentment.

Now modern marriages, partnerships, and cohabitation (or any other of the numerous terms) are more like contracts or agreements. One partner expects the other to provide equal love and support and to bring an equal amount of non-monetary value to the relationship. If this is not sustained by either party and it doesn't seem easily resolved, then there is a more ready parting of ways. Because value-depleting behavior is less tolerated in marriages and partnerships, partners with alcohol dependencies had better resolve the problem if the relationship is to survive, let alone flourish.

As you will read in the chapters ahead, though I was never violent or aggressive in any way, my wife must have nearly reached the status of sainthood by coping with some of the moods, embarrassment, and general stress I caused by my drinking habit. Though I was never given an ultimatum, I have to wonder if the strain would have eventually been too much for our relationship to survive. I can't express enough how choosing to cease drinking alcohol altogether was the best decision I have made, not only for me personally but also for the change it has made in our relationship.

I believe the same increased intolerance of excessive alcohol consumption and the antisocial and criminal behavior to which it indirectly contributes is also evident in local communities. Whereas many years ago excessive alcohol consumption and its accompanying antisocial behavior was far less common in my community, any occasional incidences were tolerated as "boys being boys" or "young people just overdoing it a bit." Now with kids starting to drink at a younger age and the increasing incidence frequency as well as the severity of the behavior and criminal actions, it is no longer tolerated. Communities have had enough and want alcohol-related inappropriate and criminal behavior more heavily policed and dealt with more harshly by the legal system.

So, regardless of whether it is business, sports, entertainment, or personal or community relationships, our modern way of life is now more than ever detrimentally affected by inappropriate alcohol consumption. We all need to make informed, rational, and clear decisions about how our lives are best served. What do we really want to get (or, more appropriately, what do we want to achieve) from this all too short time we have during our lifetime? Do we want to live life fully and experience our journey's challenges, lessons, and successes with all our senses intact and clear? Do we want to actively and purposefully participate in the creation of our desired relationships and business and personal accomplishments?

We are meant to be the creators of our life experiences and experience them with all our external and internal senses. This can happen fully only if our minds and bodies are as close to our natural state of clarity as possible. Any effects of alcohol or other drugs reduce this ability to fully appreciate what our life is really like. I for one can attest to that, as the effects of alcohol dulled the richness of my life experiences for about thirty years. Most often people with substance dependencies dull themselves purposely, rather than facing and resolving negative results naturally. Therefore they cannot completely appreciate their life experience from a holistic perspective involving their body, mind, and spirit and make fully informed decisions on how to proceed.

This is crucial because our deep internal feelings and emotions form the guidance system that tells us whether we are moving in the right direction or not. Think of them as a *lifeometer* (pronounced like "thermometer") that measures level of the congruency between our spiritual desires and intentions, and our actual thoughts and what we are physically manifesting in our lives.

LIFEOMETER

We cannot help but feel good when we are thinking or doing desirable things (things that nourish our spirit or soul); conversely, we cannot help but feel bad when we are thinking or doing things we don't desire (being greedy, selfish, and egocentric). We naturally feel good at the core of our being when we are being true to ourselves and are on the right path. When we are deeply feeling anything else (other than good), then a course adjustment or a change of thinking is required.

Alcohol and drugs interfere with our body, thoughts, and core emotions, and our true way forward becomes lost. People with an alcohol habit are living a life of avoidance with a corrupt guidance system. We get conditioned at a very early age through advertising, peer example, and general complacency to substance consumption, such that we believe we *need* to take external substances in order to deal with modern stresses and to feel good. Although my major dependence was alcohol, I personally went on to develop habits of varying levels with smoking, gambling, and drug use, all in an attempt to make me feel better in some way. Regardless of whether people use alcohol, another substance, or other vice that serves to mask their true feelings, they will never be in touch with their real selves and live the lives they desire until they permanently resolve that habit.

The winners and the successful people in today's world will be those whose intentions and reality are highly congruent. They continually seek the best from themselves, living life with passion, belief, and commitment. They actively create their own future by pushing beyond their current boundaries and trying new things. These people don't want to play the victim or settle for what currently is if it is not serving them well. Winners acknowledge that they will be confronted by serious challenges along life's journey and don't let these challenges disempower them. They have an internal locus of control and generate their sense of self-worth and power by focusing on their own values and behaviors, not those of others with lesser standards. They use all their senses to experience feedback from their actions and environment, and then use their emotional guidance system (lifeometer) to make a decision about the way forward.

These people want to live fully and see no benefit from clouding their minds and body with the delusions that alcohol creates. For a few generations now too many societies have developed a culture of "Don't worry, she'll be right, mate; someone else will look after us if we fall on hard times." We've become soft and the masses have stopped taking responsibility for their own actions, outcomes, and solutions. They rely on family, the community, and government to be a safety net and to fix all their problems. Globally people have denied their responsibility to control their own success and satisfaction and want others to provide their desires for them. How many times would you have heard someone complaining about the meagerness of a community or government handout when they themselves aren't contributing or adding value to the community in any way? We have become largely a spoon-fed society.

Winners don't want to rely on others for their happiness and success. They accept responsibility for their present circumstances and future results. They acknowledge it takes personal effort and contributing value to others before they have earned the right of both emotional and material reward. Winners relish being in control of their own destiny.

The losers in our modern world will be those who live in fear of stepping outside of their comfort zone. They also let the emotional pain (feedback) of negative earlier life experiences prevent them from trying to push their boundaries again for fear of more pain. Instead of using the feedback to reassess their way forward, they attempt to erase the emotional pain by using external substances they believe will make them feel better. Losers readily adopt a victim mentality and release themselves from being responsible for their happiness and success. They hide from any responsibility and readily blame others for their situation. Losers place greater value on what others think of them than on what they think of themselves. They hand their power over to others instead of drawing on their own values and creative desires to govern their actions.

Alcohol is the most common legal substance that helps them deal with their ineptness. Of course, the emotional feedback life provides us is there for a reason and doesn't get deleted by consuming external substances. Alcohol merely acts as a mask and only serves to temporarily affect people's perception, and they think things are better (because they don't feel as bad) only while intoxicated. If people use alcohol to relieve emotional pain they are sensing, they will have to keep regularly topping up to keep masking and pushing the unpleasant emotions down. It is a no-win situation, as the person develops a habit and dependence on alcohol. The original emotional feedback is still there and apparent when sober, while new alcohol-related problems are added to the mix.

People who use alcohol just to feel good are in a similar situation. If they're using alcohol to feel good, that must mean they aren't feeling good normally and want to change that. As before, the reason they aren't feeling good in the first place doesn't go away. The alcohol just depresses the nervous system enough so that they perceive they are feeling better. It is my understanding that people who are very unhappy before they drink alcohol don't suddenly get significantly happier. Due to the effect alcohol has on the brain and nervous system, they will lose some inhibitions and feel different, which may seem funny and cause them to experience their feelings differently. However, alcohol is a nervous system depressant, not a stimulant. I'm sure most people have heard the saying someone was "crying drunk," highlighting its depressive nature. Alcohol doesn't change an unhappy situation into a happy one. It is a chemical that changes your brain and perception of reality, which can have far greater negative consequences than just the temporary delusion.

As for the people trying to escape from painful emotional feedback and the ones that are just trying to feel better emotionally, they all end up in the same misguided boat. Alcohol is not going to make their lives better. It is not going to change the important feedback that their emotional guidance system is appropriately giving them. It will not provide them with a solution to life's challenges. It can only detract from their real experience of life and will throw in a whole stack of other alcohol-related problems on top of the ones they are trying to avoid. People with an alcohol habit will lose.

Believe me, it is not my intention to be harsh. I spent more than thirty years of my life rowing that misguided boat. For most of that time I did not fully understand why I was reliant on alcohol, or even appreciate just how much I was dependent on it. In the next chapter, I'll talk more about this part of my life. For more than half of it I knew I was not living my life anywhere near my full potential, and certainly not the life of creativity and adventure I had daydreamed about as a young boy. Sure, through a process of effort, trials, and tribulations, I had I found myself in a position where I had a good job and a family that loved each other. However, all facets of my life would have been so much better and more fulfilling if I never had an alcohol habit. I had settled into a comfortable pattern where drinking was the normal routine. Perhaps for many of you reading this, alcohol consumption is also so engrained in your way of life you perceive it is part of who you are—regardless of the negative consequences and limiting effects it has on your life and the lives around you.

So before we go into the Alcohemy process step-by-step, I'd like to tell you a little bit about my journey. My hope is that it will be obvious that if I can become completely and happily alcohol-free, you or your loved one can too. No matter how much you believe it right now, I am telling you there is not one person on this planet who *needs* alcohol in their life and who wouldn't be better off without it. My biggest hurdle was to actually believe life would somehow be better if I didn't drink alcohol at all (to me that simply did not compute).

For those who don't have an alcohol habit, my intent in the next chapter is for you to understand not only the effects suffered by loved ones, friends, and acquaintances of those with the habit, but just how deeply painful and humiliating it can be for the ones with the habit themselves.

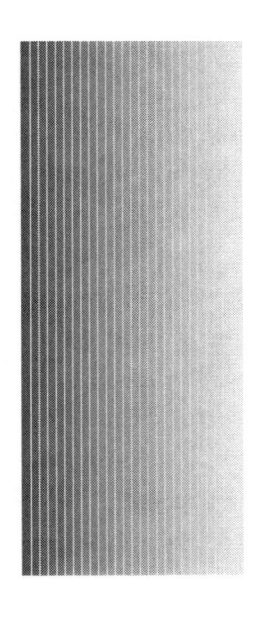

CHAPTER 2

MY PERSONAL STRUGGLE WITH ALCOHOL DEPENDENCY

Although your personal story will be different, I'd like to share with you the genuine struggle and frustration that alcohol caused me and people around me. This directly relates to me reaching the tipping point that caused me to develop my way of becoming permanently alcohol-free. As you will realize later, understanding why I started to drink and why I desperately wanted to stop was a crucial element in Alcohemy's recipe of success. As you progress through my journey, I want you to relate it to similar experiences of struggle that you have had to go through. For people reading this who don't have an alcohol or substance dependency, I invite you to relate the struggle of my journey to someone you know who has.

I am taking the liberty over the next three chapters to be quite detailed about my past as it relates to my alcohol dependency (and how I discovered the solution) so that the details may spark realizations and connections between your own past experiences and an alcohol habit. In Element 1, you will need to do the same kind of detailed review of your own life as the first step in the Alcohemy process.

However, some of you may not want to take the time to read through my own experience and just want to get straight to the practical process. If this is so, please feel free to skip straight to Element 1 and begin the process for yourself.

But if you're not quite sure where to begin, I invite you to join me as I recount parts of my own journey. Sometimes it is quite difficult to see how alcohol is damaging your own life and the relationships around you until you see similar symptoms reflected back to you in someone else's life. My life has by no means been heroic or even necessarily worse than most. But going through the Alcohemy process will be so much more effective if you are already convinced of your need to cease your alcohol habit, and my hope is that my own detailed story will spark that for you in some small way.

I was born in 1959 in the very small country town of Monto in Queensland, Australia. My family (father, mother, older sister, and younger brother) owned and lived on a 1,220 hectare (3,015 acre) out-of-the-way cattle-grazing property called Coolamondah at the very dead end of a winding dirt road thirty kilometers (nineteen miles) from town. Our property was hilly country, and most of the once thick forest and scrub had gradually been cleared from a fair bit of it to make way for hilly grazing land for our beef cattle (and dairy cattle in the early days). It was considered fairly rough country and especially harsh during drought times when the expected summer rains didn't come and the property turned a dusty brown. During these years we had to supply our cattle supplementary feed of hay and molasses/urea licks on a weekly basis, as well as cut down bottle trees for them to feed on the leaves and moist trunk fiber. But during good seasons it produced hills and valleys of lush Green Panic and Rhodes grasses for grazing, and the cattle were easily well fattened.

I was the middle child of three, having an elder sister and younger brother. Ours was a family-run property, and we were all expected to help out with as many chores as possible from a very young age. Being the eldest boy I was expected to develop my skills as early as possible. As soon as I could be taught to do something to work on the property, I was. I can vividly recall driving the work truck by sliding off the seat to operate the clutch to change gears and then sliding back up to see where I was steering. I learned to ride a horse when I could balance well enough to stay on top without falling off. After a few years of learning the hard way, by being thrown from bucking or bolting horses and spending weekends helping mustering on our hilly property, I became a very skilled horseman. In fact, I recall my father likening my horse-riding skills to that famous Man from Snowy River in the poem of the same name by Banjo Paterson. I fondly remember him bestowing praise on me after one three-day mustering stint of the particularly rugged 400 hectare (988 acre) paddock on our neighbor's property. Their cattle were wilder than ours, and their property even more hilly and rugged, so it took some serious riding and mustering skills to round up all their cattle. Those were long, hard days for a young lad, as we saddled up and left our property at first light and often rode back well after dark.

Being born and raised on a remote rural property, we also used to shoot wild animals and birds that competed for grazing grass or crops (kangaroos, wallabies, rabbits/hares), threatened and attacked livestock (dingoes), ate our grain crops (parrots, cockatoos, etc.), served as our own food (pigeons, scrub turkeys), or provided meat to feed our cattle dogs. I remember saving money from work and buying my first air rifle when I turned ten, and I started using the other higher-powered rifles soon after that. It was another skill I could use to help out, and I soon became quite an accomplished animal tracker and marksman. I'm not trying to imply I was some unique legend by working hard as a young kid and being good at most things I turned my hand to. It was the life and way of the land; every country kid who lived on a property had to toughen up and master as much as possible as soon as possible to be a work asset.

Everyone's circumstances in life are uniquely different. The personal perceptions we formed, what they meant to us, and how we adapted to those circumstances are more important than the circumstances themselves. My early memories of life on the land and growing up on this isolated property combined to leave me with a strong internal sense of hardship and loneliness. We were always fighting to make financial ends meet. I recall my father always stating we barely made enough money to pay the large repayment on our bank loan—and some years we didn't and had to borrow more money. Any profit went straight back into property, equipment repairs, or necessary improvements to the property, like building a new dam for water or clearing more scrub to increase grass for the cattle. We could afford to buy only the bare essentials for living and went without what many people now take for granted. When we were young, we didn't wear shoes around the property or to school either. The soles of our feet became so hard that sharp burs and prickles rarely penetrated.

My father worked from before daylight until after dark, and as young kids we also worked hard before and after school and on weekends on numerous jobs to help run the property. It was rare that we had free time to perhaps visit a schoolmate's place for the weekend or have a friend over to our place, and even then work had to come first. At the time, even though we kids may have felt deprived of the material things we would have loved to have, I realized both my parents would have provided more if they felt they could have afforded it. Instead, we kids were allowed to choose a young calf each year as payment for all the work we did. After several years, when it had grown, we sold it to the abattoir and could keep the proceeds. I saved any money I earned and paid for things like tennis rackets, cricket equipment, our first pushbike, and then, when I was older, a small farm motorbike. My father was raised the tough country way of hard work and going without; therefore so were we. I guess you could say we were brought up with *tough love*, though it felt like the *love* part was missing and it was just *tough*.

On reflection, though, it was not so much material possessions my heart longed for most over those years. It was the lack of an expression of love and affection, a happy family, and excitement and adventure. Together with the unrelenting hard work, loneliness, and (what I considered unjust) harsh discipline, I remember a distinct inner feeling of deep sadness and desperation. I wanted to be happy and to enjoy life, but my circumstances just didn't seem to provide much opportunity.

However, despite this being the perception of my childhood, I can now say that I am grateful to have been raised on that cattle property and to have had those experiences. Without them I would not have been on the journey I have, learned important lessons along the way, or become the person I am now, in a position to share my advice and make a difference for others.

The isolation and struggle of living on our rural property, combined with serious marital relationship issues, saw my mother separate from my father. I was about twelve years old when she moved off the property to live in Monto, where she worked as a nursing sister at the local hospital. I was told sometime later that she would have left years earlier but waited until we children were old enough to understand what was happening. I can still clearly recall crying my eyes out, asking why they couldn't just sort things out and stay together. Being very innocent-minded and naïve, I didn't realize that parents could split up; I had not been exposed to it nor seen it happen with any of my friends' families. To make things worse, my sister also left with Mum at this time to live with her in town, since this was where she attended high school. It is difficult even as an adult now to put into words how I felt at the time. My thoughts were jumbled, my heart was breaking, and I just couldn't imagine what the future would be like with a broken family. I just wanted everyone to be happy.

This wasn't to be, and my brother and I remained to help my father run the property, in addition to doing the housework and getting ourselves off to school each day. My mother's leaving was very traumatic even for quite some time afterward, as it was not a mutually agreed-upon separation. There was a lot of bitterness between the two, and my father's emotions fluctuated from very upset to very angry. To make matters worse, like in most country communities, everyone in our community knew each other and each other's business. The local courier who delivered our mail and fuel and picked up produce was also a friend and gossip source to all the property families. I remember it was extremely upsetting for all of us involved when he came to pick up some of the larger items Mum and my sister were taking with them.

Over the following years, when I felt brave enough to spent time to reflect on it, I understood why she'd left, and after some years passed

I came to accept it. As an example, when reflecting back, I often used to be amazed (and a bit embarrassed) when I visited school friends' places and saw their parents showing obvious signs of affection for each other (like having a hug or kiss, or snuggling close on the lounge when watching TV at night) and calling each other names like "Honey" or "Love." I cannot recall ever seeing my parents do or say anything like that or show any signs of affection toward each other. In fact, most of my memories of their relationship were of arguing, general disharmony, or indifference. Furthermore, there were a few significantly horrific incidents I saw and overheard that no young child (or adult for that matter) should ever have to witness involving any couple, let alone their own parents. These memories, though less painful now, will stay with me forever. For many years into my adulthood, every time these memories entered my consciousness I would immediately block them with other thoughts. I would actively instruct myself to erase these memories from my mind, though I was never successful. I would just force myself to override them with other thoughts. Eventually, during my reflection upon my childhood as an adult, I came to see my parents' relationship as very much doomed beyond repair and can now see it was appropriate that they did separate.

Even in the midst of the struggle and trauma, a brighter side of my childhood was that I loved the rolling hills, valleys, and rugged landscape that made up our grazing property. From the dense scrub that was still standing on the outlying or hard to access areas, to the steep slopes of the old, long extinct, red-soiled volcano that bordered one side of our secluded property, our land provided great adventures of discovery for a young boy. During the times when I wasn't required to be working on regular tasks (such as fencing, mustering, plowing fields, etc.), I would seek out and travel into these isolated areas. I also walked through these rugged areas of our property when I was on solo hunting treks to shoot wallabies for our cattle dogs' food. I used to imagine (probably quite correctly) that no person had ever set foot on some of the places I walked. (Well, at least white Australian footsteps anyway, as in some of the areas I traveled I would find ancient Aboriginal artifacts such as stone axes and chopped toe-holds in dead tree trunks where Aborigines had climbed in search of honey from wild beehives.)

I really enjoyed these solo excursions and the great feeling of adventure and discovery they gave me. I loved the sense of freedom and being part of nature in all its glory and harshness. I felt very much at home and at peace wandering through these remote areas with just my thoughts and imagination for company. Whenever I had the opportunity I loved to read stories of adventure and discovery, such as journeys to the South Pole, forays into the Amazon jungles, exploration of Egyptian pyramids and pharaohs' tombs, discoveries of ancient civilizations like the ruins of Machu Picchu in Peru (where I actually visited recently), pioneering and settlement of continents like Australia, America, and Europe, and other great feats of adventure and discovery around the world. These treks of mine were like mini-expeditions in which I was traveling solo into uncharted lands to make my own great discoveries.

In my preteen and early teenage years, I began to perceive the discipline applied to us kids as decidedly harsh. If we didn't deliver on our obligations, or behaved in any way that was deemed inappropriate, then we copped a belting. This was usually metered out via a flexible switchy stick, piece of rubber hose, leather belt, flyswatter, or whatever other item was suitable and close at hand. At times I was even made to go and select my own switchy stick to be hit with, and if it wasn't deemed good enough then I got twice as much punishment. I can still remember the fear we felt when one of us knew we were going to cop a belting over some error.

Kids are kids and I was no different, definitely deserving some of my punishment. I recall one such time when, at a very young age, I zapped my younger brother with a cattle jigger. This is a long narrow plastic tube filled with large batteries that delivered a significant shock when the two prongs at one end were pressed against a cattle hide. It was used to keep stubborn cattle moving along narrow cattle yard walkways. I can't remember why, but for some reason I thought it appropriate to deliver one of these shocks to my younger brother when he wasn't looking. After he went crying to our father, Dad applied the "eye for an eye" rule. In the end I don't recall whether it was my brother or my father who did the deed, though I had to go and get the jigger and stand there while I was given the full force of the shock. I was only young myself and remember crying my eyes out, saying I was very sorry and begging him not to do it.

Can you remember a time when you had done something clearly wrong, but the gravity of the situation and the remorse you felt were so apparent that you quickly learned your lesson without the need for any punishment? This was one of those times. Needless to say, the punishment was carried out, and it was a hard lesson learned. Though some may have been deserved, I don't believe others, like leaving my school jumper at primary school, warranted the belting I got for them.

Looking back on it now, any one isolated incident would not appear too distressing to me or anyone else. But when everything was thrown into the mix, I felt very unhappy a lot of the time. This feeling of despair would build up at times to a fairly serious level. I can't remember if particular events triggered it, though I suspect it was usually the culmination of several issues at once that would put me in such a depressed state. I clearly remember more than once going on one of my hunting treks and considering shooting myself while I was out there. When I was out wandering the ranges on my own, I felt free, with a sense of peace, adventure, and being in control. The thought of returning home to me felt like returning to harshness and heartache. I certainly didn't have any mature coping skills or support mechanism to fall back on, so I can only deduce that my spirit's innate desire to live this life and a subconscious core knowing that I would end up okay prevented me from ending it. I guess my desire for life and trusting that I would someday fulfill my desire for adventure, discovery, and happiness won the inner debate. But all this set the stage for a deep need that made me quite susceptible to an alcohol dependency later.

Don't get me wrong: not every childhood memory I had was bad, though there were times I can remember hating my father—so much so that I distinctly recall thinking, *When I get old enough, I'm going to give you such a huge belting with my fists as payback.* This nearly came to pass actually in my early teens. One time I stepped between my father and my brother when my father was administering a beating and told him to stop, as it was too much. I can't recall whether he went to push me out of the way, though I put my fists up as a sign I was determined to stop him hurting my brother any more. This proved fruitless, as Dad had trained in boxing in his Air Force days. He proceeded to punch me backward all the way down our house's hallway into my room. At least he left my brother alone. It wasn't very long after this that I'd finally had enough and left the property and moved into town to live with my mother.

This move, though a welcome change from the isolation and hard work of living on the remote property, brought with it new challenges (or I should say "temptations"). I was progressing through puberty, was good at the many sports I competed in, and was above average academically. I grew my blond hair longer than my mother would have preferred (as it was the emerging fashion of the day), and certainly longer than our high school regulations permitted. I think my mother let me get away with it as maybe some sort of compensation for harsh years I had been through, including the trauma of my parents' separation. I was also becoming popular with schoolmates, including ones older than me. This popularity meant a great deal to me as I was the youngest and shortest of my class, and having this popularity gave me advantages over some of the bigger, older, and less popular kids at high school.

Having said that, even though I was small in stature, I had a big heart and would always feel strong empathy for other kids that were unfairly treated or picked on. I would find myself stepping in to help kids in this situation, regardless of whether the offenders were bigger than me. I stood up for what I believed was right, and at times my popular status may have prevented a few more serious altercations. Even though I was strong and tough for my size (because of years of hard physical work on the property), it was good to know that other older and popular kids also had my back if I needed them. I guess I had a deep intrinsic sense of what I felt was right and wrong from a very early age. Though over the years my alcohol consumption may have affected that sense on occasions, my desire to always do the right thing has remained as a central part of my character.

These high school social bonds soon extended to young adults outside of school, as now that I lived in town I had the opportunity to mix with other people. Before moving to town my social life outside of school was nonexistent, except for some sports events or the rare visit to a mate's property on a weekend. It was like a kid's first visit into a candy shop: I wanted as much as I could get. Though now mixing with some young adults outside the scrutiny of parents or the school environment brought me into ready contact with alcohol and cigarettes. It was from this point I started my decline into dependency on both these habits.

My Journey to the Dark Side
Alcohol exposure was infrequent in my early years, having been raised on an isolated cattle property by parents who hardly ever drank. Regardless, being very young and impressionable, any exposure creates perceptions in our forming minds of what alcohol is used for and how acceptable it is in our everyday life. Harmful beliefs will be formed if exposed to inappropriate alcohol use by influential sources (usually family and media), especially in the absence of any evidence of significant negative consequences. If during teenage and young adult years unsuitable beliefs are combined with access to alcohol, a strong desire to feel better, and inadequate skills to achieve this in a healthy way, then the start of a dependence on alcohol is a very likely outcome.

When I permanently moved from the property into town, the opportunity to access alcohol significantly increased. I was a fairly innocent boy from the bush, suddenly mixing with more astute town kids and young adults. I remember that my first drinking session after moving into town was when I was supposed to be at the local cinema one weekend night. Instead a mate and I got one of the older lads to buy us a couple of stubbies of beer and we drank them in an old shed in the lane behind the main street. The older lads we were with were considered to be the toughest in town, so this was like being accepted to the big leagues. I remember being told if we drank it faster it would have a greater effect. The feeling was a mixture of excitement of doing something more adult and fear of getting caught.

Any rare sip of alcohol I had as a child was simply defined by its horrible taste. But by this age I definitely perceived the pleasant, intoxicating effect of alcohol as a benefit. It would be a good replacement for the feelings of struggle and harshness of my younger years, the memories and still ongoing difficulties of my parents' separation, and my own struggle to make a name for myself as I continued through puberty and high school. I would still go out to the property some weekends to give Dad and my brother a hand with big jobs like mustering cattle, though during these times I would usually get lots of questions about Mum. I just wanted it to all go away and to feel happy as much as possible. I used to look forward to the occasions when I could be alone with my girlfriend or, if I couldn't be with her, then with mates and/or consuming alcohol. There were still a few times when I could enjoy some quiet solitude and immerse myself in thoughts of mystic or exciting adventures and discoveries, and going on to do great deeds in the world. However these thoughts now had to compete against the ones of quiet despair based on my past experiences and the new activity going on in my life now.

During the rest of my high school years, on many occasions I drank alcohol on weekends with school mates and young adults from around the local region. Monto was a country town where a lot of first-year teachers were sent, so we had a lot of young single teachers at that time. Some of them were only three to five years older than us, and Monto can be a boring place to live for young city people. It was only logical that some of us older high school kids became friends with the younger teachers outside of school and used to play sports and socialize together. Short- and long-term romances even occurred between young teachers and older students, though I won't elaborate on those details. It will suffice to say out of the many parties over my last year at high school, some involved teachers, and I have some very fond memories of them that still make me smile.

However, I can remember a particular time during my eleventh-grade year when we had a party at the house some of the young single teachers rented. It was a twenty-first birthday party for one of the female teachers, and it was the first time I had drunk vodka and orange juice. It tasted so good that I had way too much and ended up drunk and violently sick. I passed out on the backseat of an older mate's car. He came out later that night after the party had finished to take me home, and found I had vomited all over his backseat and floor. He was very upset and I was very embarrassed, as that was the first time I had been so drunk that I had no recollection of doing what I did.

Also during my eleventh grade year at Monto, I decided to apply to college to complete an associate diploma in stock and meat inspection beginning the following year. As I only needed my year 10 grades to qualify for college entry, my interest in my final high school year diminished and weekend alcohol consumption became more frequent. My new social life and drinking habits indirectly caused relationship problems between me and my girlfriend of three years, and we eventually broke up toward the end of the year. I remember being heartbroken that she didn't want to be with me anymore; being so wrapped up in my new existence and thinking more about myself, I guess I couldn't see what effect my behavior was having on others. My perception was that compared to my life out on the property, these last few years of senior high school with more freedom were the best.

I attended parties most weekends, where I would always have alcohol. Even at the weekly night tennis competition I played in we would occasionally sneakily have a beer in a mate's car at the end before walking or being driven home. Without the stabilizing influence of my long-term girlfriend I would seek happiness from being as socially active as I could, and in a small country town that involved alcohol. It seems clear to me now that I was showing the early signs of depending on the effects of alcohol to feel good even at that age. Furthermore, for a fifteen-year-old I was drinking way too often and way too much each time. Alcohol provided an escape from my old world of harshness and heartache out on the property, and I was trying to erase as much of that as possible from my memory. How I achieved that didn't really matter to me at the time, as I was in a desperate hurry to leave that childhood behind and live in an adult world where I felt I would have control over my circumstances. I wanted to be the master of my own destiny.

I had only just turned sixteen when I left Monto and went off to college to study animal husbandry and livestock inspection. As far as my perceived social status went, instead of a big fish in a small country town pond, I became a young small fish in a big college pond. For the first few years I lived on campus, as I neither had a driver's license nor could I afford to pay rent for a shared flat. Even though the legal drinking age was eighteen, there was no rigorous policing of this on campus. Alcohol seemed to flow freely for those who could afford it and were discreet enough not to draw undue attention. There were always some private or student-organized parties to attend, or I would simply get together with mates for a drink in someone's room. I was young, and without the steadying influence of a regular girlfriend, I partied as often as I could afford. Consequently my drinking habit gradually increased at college over the next few years to the stage where it was affecting my desire to complete assignments on time and even attend some lectures. Depending on the occasion, some midweek drinking sessions would go late into the night and I would miss the odd first-up morning lecture.

At college we had a total of sixteen weeks of student leave spread throughout each year. Over the five years I spent at college I would regularly travel home to Monto during these vacation breaks. Back home it would be a mix of working on the property to earn some more spending money and partying on weekends with mates still living in the area.

In small country towns like Monto (as it would be in many rural Australian communities) drinking alcohol was just what people did. In fact, you would be hard-pressed to find many non-alcohol-drinking males in rural communities and townships. A lot of townsfolk would go to their favorite hotel or club after work for a few drinks and spend even more time there on weekends. The men who lived on properties would go to the hotel after stock sale days or on any occasion they had reason to come into town. This habit is passed down from generation to generation: as young kids they would have witnessed their fathers performing this ritual, just as their children would witness them. It was as much a rural social event as it was to wash away the stress of the hard work and financial struggle with a few drinks. For the younger blokes it was an opportunity not only to relax from hard work but also to showcase their wits and bravado against the other young men and maybe build a popular reputation that the young women would notice. There is no doubt that rural country living is often hard and stressful (as rural suicide rates reflect), and it is just the way of country life to use alcohol as a remedy for temporary relief. So drinking alcohol was not only a widely accepted habit but virtually an expectation. Unfortunately, knowledge and skill in using positive alternative methods for stress prevention and relief seem particularly lacking in rural communities and do not get passed from generation to generation.

It was at one of my college semester breaks that I recall a particularly disturbing alcohol-related incident that troubled me for a long time. I was at a bonfire birthday party for a friend from high school. I'd had a fair bit to drink and I was mucking around wrestling with my younger brother when I put him in a headlock. Little did I realize that I was gripping him around his throat too tightly, which stopped his breathing and began to choke him. When I released him he was gasping for air, nearly in tears, and of course extremely angry with me. I asked him only a few years ago if he remembered it, and thankfully he said he couldn't. I have not forgotten it, though, because once sober I was ashamed I had done something while affected by alcohol that really hurt and could have killed my brother, whom I loved. It also may have been one of the first times I became aware that there were serious negative side effects to drinking too much, apart from just feeling sick and hungover. Still, I rationalized it away with thoughts like *Everyone does silly things occasionally when they drink too much* and *I've learned from that and it won't happen again*, as I don't believe the incident had any long-lasting effect on my desire to drink alcohol. At most I would have thought, *I'll be careful not to drink too much in the future.*

But where is the boundary between having enough and having too much? Reflecting upon my life, I now realize this had always been a problem for me. I knew that I had less physical tolerance for alcohol than most of my mates because of my smaller stature. Even today I am only 171 centimeters (just over five foot seven) and 72 kilograms (159 pounds), and because I was a late developer, I was shorter and much lighter back then.

Nevertheless, all my life I have been told I that am an intelligent, deep-thinking person with an analytical mind. For the life of me I could not work out why I couldn't determine when I had a sufficient amount of alcohol to drink, even if it was less than others around me. As a rationally thinking, intelligent person, I should be able to stop before I had too much and behaved badly, before I (and others) suffered the consequences. Over the years I had become a seasoned drinker, therefore I reasoned my tolerance should have increased to a high degree and I should not be getting drunk so easily. It was true that I could handle more alcohol than a novice or non-drinker, but not as much as other males I usually drank socially with—but the magical, appropriate stop point of when I personally had had enough to drink seemed forever elusive to me.

I now understand from studying medical and other alcohol-related research material that quite a few factors affect one's level of alcohol intoxication, therefore influencing where that stop point may be. A key finding was that our thought, judgment, and reasoning capacity is one of the first areas to be affected by alcohol and occurs between as little as 0.01–0.06 percent blood alcohol content (BAC). This is just one or two standard alcoholic drinks for most people. Therefore, after even one or two drinks, our decisions are often not based on reality, but rather our perhaps significantly skewed perceptions of it. It then makes perfect sense that with each swallow of alcohol, our perception of when we have had enough will also change.

When making our own subjective analysis of when to stop drinking (based on how we are feeling), there can be no objective and fixed thin gray line for us to use as a "stop drinking right now" point. I call it a thin gray line because (1) gray is somewhere between black and white, or what we feel is wrong and right, and (2) it is thin because it is very easy to miss, and one extra drink, or even less, is all it can take for some to have already stepped over it.

I believe each of us has a thin gray line that is our "stop drinking right now" point, and in a sober, clear-headed, and composed state of mind, this line is placed in a position relative to our core beliefs and values. For some this is abstinence from alcohol altogether, while others don't appear to set any limits on what they deem acceptable behavior for themselves, even when sober. One thing I am certain of, though, is that no matter where your original thin gray line is placed, its substance dissolves the moment it comes into contact with alcohol. And the more alcohol applied, the more rapidly it dissolves. If you drink alcohol, I bet you can remember a time when before drinking you had set some firm boundaries on what you would (or wouldn't) do, only to have that decision change after you have had a few drinks. You were more easily persuaded by others, or convinced yourself that it was okay to change your mind, to do or say something that you had previously decided not to.

At typical teenage and young adult parties (like the one where I hurt my brother), where the expectation is to get intoxicated and experience an altered state of mind as part of the high, it is little wonder that accidents such as that happen. It is only after we are again sober and our rational and proper judgment has returned that we see the stupidity of some of the actions that took place. It is quite clear to see how the rational mind is affected if you have been completely sober at a party where others are at various stage of intoxication. You get to witness and appreciate how your friends' behavior can change so dramatically from their normal personalities. What appears to the sober observer as embarrassing or even unacceptable behavior can to most of the alcohol-affected partygoers appear as just funny and quite okay. Even if the intoxicated person still recognizes that certain behavior is embarrassing or improper, the "care factor" is usually reduced, as the loss of inhibitions is also one of the first personality trait changes to be observed after alcohol consumption.

The New Normal

Between partying at college and partying when I came home to Monto during semester breaks, I was well and truly cementing in my alcohol drinking habit. Alcohol provided me a badge of developing manhood and social acceptance, a sense of euphoria and relief from the stressful memories of childhood I was desperately trying to leave behind, and an ability to mask the ongoing perceived feelings of academic hardship and high expectations that go with being a young teenager in an adult college. Because I believed I was getting all these great benefits from drinking alcohol, both at and away from college, the frequency and amount consumed steadily increased.

But so did the harmful consequences. One of many low points as a consequence of my drinking (and one I was very ashamed of) was during another college break back in Monto after an evening drinking session.

A few young local mates and I made a regrettable decision to break into a local club and steal a few bottles of alcohol to drink. I guess we must have all been broke and wanted to continue partying. We removed some louvers to gain access to the inside and replaced them after exiting so that no one would immediately know that we were in there. We figured they would notice the alcohol was gone only at inventory time, perhaps some time later. However, the next morning I could not find my wallet and by then was not only ashamed at what I had done but panicking that my wallet had fallen from my rear pocket while we were inside the club building. My wallet had my driver's license and other identifying material in it, so as I rarely ever went to that club, I would have been questioned as to how my wallet got there (perhaps even behind the bar area or near the storeroom). Even though I believe we took only one bottle, after finding my wallet they would have surely then noticed the missing spirit and I would have been arrested. I was virtually sick from worry this was about to happen.

Up until then I may have done some stupid things while affected by alcohol, though I had never accepted or condoned the idea of stealing anything. From a young age I considered myself honest, trustworthy, well-mannered, and respectful to others. I always had to work very hard to earn the money I got to buy the things I wanted. My brother and I pitched in together to buy our first pushbike and our own motorbikes for farm work and to ride the few kilometers to where we caught the school bus. I paid for my first proper tennis racket, cricket bat, and air rifle out of money I had earned. The decision to participate in the club break-in incident was affected not only *by* alcohol, but also by the desire *for* alcohol and to fit in with other young mates with a similar mindset.

So here I was the morning after stealing alcohol from the club, terrified I was about to get arrested for doing something I intrinsically knew was very wrong and should have had the guts to not have been a part of. Out of sheer desperation and wishful thinking I went to our mate's place where we drank the stolen alcohol to see if my wallet was there, which it wasn't. Then again out of desperation I rang the other mate whose car we had been in to see if by a remote chance it may have been in it (though I don't recall ever taking it out of my jeans pocket). To my absolute elation it was found lodged in the crevice of the backseat of the car where I had been sitting. I cannot begin to describe how absolutely relieved I was, and I swore I would never consider stealing anything ever again. This experience became such a powerful confirmation that stealing (or wrongfully gaining anything) was not something I wanted to be involved in. To this day even if I notice I'm being given too much change for an item I have purchased, I will let the cashier know and hand back the excess change. By the way, since that incident I did make a generous recompense to the club, not only to do the right thing but also help appease my conscience.

However, as my subsequent stories will attest to, even though I may have never stolen anything again, I went on to lead a life that would have scored dramatically low on the lifeometer I presented in chapter 1. Due to alcohol-affected decisions, my actions deviated greatly from my internal values and beliefs time after time.

When I got my motorbike license (at seventeen years old), in addition to travelling the five and a half hours home from college to Monto for some weekend parties, I would often travel an hour and a half to Brisbane (the capital of our state, Queensland) some weekends to party with friends there. Even though I was not eighteen years old (the legal drinking age), I would get into pubs and nightclubs with a fake student ID card. By then I was drinking spirits whenever I could afford it, though, as most of my college days were financially impoverished, beer and cider were more affordable and usually the drinks of choice.

This alcohol-fueled lifestyle had obvious effects on my relationships and productivity, and endangered my life in no uncertain terms. One rainy night back in Monto on the way to a party, I crashed a motorbike I was riding over an embankment and headfirst into a railway track, breaking both my collarbone and leg. The rain had been stinging my eyes, causing me to squint, and in the poorly lit conditions I missed a sharp corner and went off the road and over into the railway cutting. The mate who owned the bike was my pillion passenger, and he broke his wrist when he flew over my back on impact and into the ground. I was unconscious for a while, as I had smashed my helmet and head on the steel train track.

Other mates in a panel van traveling ahead of us noticed we had stopped following them and returned to search for us. They took us to the local ambulance station, from where we were taken to the hospital. My mother, who was a nursing sister at the hospital (and happened to be on duty that night), asked me if I had been drinking. I told her we were on the way to a party, therefore I had *only* had about a six-pack of beer (which in those times for me wasn't a large amount). She was shocked and disappointed that I had put myself and others at risk and reminded me that if the accident was reported to the police and I was blood-tested, I would lose my driver's license.

About a year later, during another one of my college holiday breaks back in Monto, I was indeed apprehended by the local police officer for what is called drink driving in Australia. A few mates and I had been drinking most of the afternoon at a local pub and I had not planned to be driving. My mate had driven us that evening to a cabaret at a nearby township hotel. When it came time to leave late that night he was literally too drunk to drive, so I thought I would be the one to save the day and drive us home to Monto. Drink driving was still commonplace in rural towns in those times (late 1970s) and laws against it were not heavily enforced. Regardless of the reason, I should not have driven. It was a case of having way too much alcohol to drink, and my judgment and reasoning were grossly affected. Even though I knew I had consumed way too much alcohol to legally drive, I still believed I could physically drive quite okay.

It was after I had driven him the thirteen kilometers (eight miles) back to Monto that I was pulled over in the town's main street after some other local lads were making a disturbance in that area. The fact that the same police officer who stopped me had been drinking rum that night at the cabaret with the hotel owner did nothing to influence his tolerance. Further proof of my intoxication and flawed decision making was that my blood test registered 0.232 BAC, I lost my license for nine months and was fined A$900—a very large amount of money back then.

With alcohol-related incidents mounting, I began to realize the frequency and amount of alcohol I was drinking was becoming a serious problem. With each passing semester I could see my grades declining. I knew this had to do with my partying lifestyle and the amount of alcohol I was drinking.

It was a rude awakening when I failed the first semester's exams in what was supposed to be my fourth and final year. My parents were disappointed, and it was embarrassing to tell my friends back home that I had failed my college exams.

I was nineteen years old with no other career prospects, so I decided to spend the next seven months working on our cattle property at Monto and then return to redo my final college year. During those seven months at home I worked hard during the week on the cattle property and partied even harder in town on the weekends.

The early warning signs leading up to my full-on dependency are all plain for me to see now, though at the time it all just blurred into a continuous pattern of self-destructive alcohol consumption. I knew I shouldn't be drinking so much, but I didn't want to stop. Sometimes (during college and in later years) I was *consciously* drinking to get drunk and to forget the past and any current built-up frustrations I may have had. At other times it was an *unconscious* learned and accepted habit of just what people did to feel better. However, every time I got drunk and did or said something inappropriate (or even if I didn't and just woke up feeling hungover), I knew what I had done was wrong and regretted it. I wished to find a way to feel good all the time without alcohol or drugs. However, in the apparent absence of an alternative or any intervention, I continued to solidly cement my established alcohol habit until it would form a part of my *normal* life. I would go on to maintain a continuous cycle of getting smashed and then feeling guilty for many years.

After my seven months of working on the property and partying with my Monto friends, I returned to college for a year and successfully completed my associate diploma. After the exams I spent another few months partying with my Monto mates before starting work in Brisbane as a state government–employed meat inspector in 1981. Being a single twenty-one-year-old bloke with a regular good income, I could financially afford to drink whatever I wanted and as frequently as I wanted to.

Effects on Work

Over the next few years in Brisbane I'd regularly drink at hotels, clubs, and homes I rented with friends. There was always a social occasion to use as an excuse to drink if required, though my regular friends and I didn't need an excuse as it was the accepted thing to do for a young Aussie bloke. By this point in time I had already been conditioned (by about five years of regular drinking) to think that alcohol was necessary to feel good and achieve a sense of enjoyment. So far all of my social conditioning taught me that drinking alcohol was a very important (if not essential) ingredient to be confident, witty, worldly, and accepted as a real man in social gatherings of young to middle-aged people. In fact, the more a male seemed conditioned and comfortable consuming alcohol, the more respect or admiration he seemed to get from the others (as long as he didn't do anything too stupid). These were the beliefs I became programmed with in those earlier years, and they became normal and real to me.

But, in retrospect, my years in Brisbane after graduating also highlighted that my alcohol consumption was continuing to be a real problem. Just as I had missed early morning classes in school and did the bare minimum academically, I was taking days off work because I was hungover or going to work feeling sick and doing the very bare minimum to get through the day. If I had a particularly big night when I drank a lot in one session, I would have memory blackouts where I could not remember the last part of the evening—and on some occasions none of it.

But even though I could see it getting worse, I figured I would either grow out of it or deal with it when I was older and ready to settle down. I was in my early twenties and single and could see no real reason for taking any drastic action at that time. Therefore my solution was that I would just minimize the embarrassing incidents and keep an eye on things until I was older. Basically, I was avoiding the issue of my depending on alcohol to feel good and continued to make seemingly plausible excuses to justify my drinking habit.

When I transferred from Brisbane to Hervey Bay, my alcohol habits came with me. But as I matured and my work responsibility increased over my seventeen years with the state then the federal government (finishing as an AQIS export food standards officer), I gradually reduced the frequency of times I took off work for hangover reasons. This was not to say my drinking habit decreased, just that I picked my heavy drinking occasions more prudently.

When I took a redundancy from my government job to work with an electrical distribution company in order to avoid being transferred from Hervey Bay, where my wife and I both wanted to stay, I became even more serious about being sure hangovers did not affect my work responsibilities. If my performance at work ever suffered because of alcohol consumption, it was usually a result of work trips away from home for meetings, employee training, or workshops and the like. A group night out with colleagues for drinks, dinner, and more drinks at times turned into very late nights, where too much alcohol was consumed by most (including me). But I no longer took days off or sick leave related to alcohol consumption.

Regardless of whether I was physically affected by the aftereffects of alcohol consumption while at work, during workdays my mind would often project forward to having a relaxing drink that evening. For ethical reasons, as an employee I have never contemplated actually consuming alcohol during work hours, though most blue- and white-collar workers who have an alcohol dependency will attest that the desire for that first after-work drink often kicks in while still at work.

For me it used to start sometime after lunch, particularly if I was having a stressful day. I would start thinking, *Boy! Am I looking forward to that first glass of wine tonight.* And if it was a bad day on a Friday, I would be thinking, *I think I've earned a few extra bourbons tonight on top of the usual.* This was because of the conditioned response we develop to the trigger of stress. Using alcohol as the solution becomes a habit. With some it actually begins in the morning, and they have one or a few lunchtime alcohol "relaxers," which becomes a habit for them. Then when the brain doesn't get its expected alcohol intake response to a stress event, they can experience cravings to varying degrees. Starting to think about alcohol during your work day is a certain sign you have a dependency that needs to be addressed as a matter of urgency.

Effects on Friendships, Marriage, and Family Relationships

To properly chronicle the effects alcohol had upon my marriage and family relationships, I will need to back up a bit. After three years of living a hectic lifestyle at Hervey Bay as a single young bloke, I was very fortunate to meet and fall in love with my wife, Donna. We met through our jobs and were originally just casual friends because of this work connection. We were also both in separate relationships. As it happened we both found ourselves without a romantic partner at the same time and our relationship soon grew from friendship to romantic. We were in our mid-twenties and both felt ready to settle down into a lifelong relationship.

Up until that point, I'd had many girlfriends. Admittedly, some could hardly be classed as girlfriends as they were simply alcohol fueled one-night encounters. Some were very casual, short-term affairs, though there were a few more serious longer-term relationships. Now I was yearning for a life companion to commit to and recognized that Donna and I had similar core values and beliefs. I might have been living in the fast lane most of my adolescent life, but underneath the surface I really just wanted some enduring shared love and stability. I knew I couldn't keep going the way I was, nor did I want to.

Donna was beautiful and fun-loving. She liked a few social drinks and a party, though she rarely overdid it. She was also an extremely kind, considerate, honest, sensible, and very unselfish person. She had all that I was looking for in a partner's personality. She may not have technically been a guardian angel, but she was definitely a loving guardian companion.

The romance blossomed quickly; we became engaged about seven months after we started dating and were married nine months later. Donna quickly made some good friends from my soccer group and their partners during our dating and engagement, so for the first few years of marriage we both continued the social and party routine I had already established.

Drinking alcohol was now no longer a conscious way to overcome the emotional pains of childhood or a rite of passage into manhood. It was a firmly entrenched way of life for me. It was just something I did—though, yes, I also used it to make me feel better in times of stress, a practice I had learned and continued since my teenage years.

Even as an adult, there was also still an element of fitting in with the social and athletic people I was friends with. The mates I socialized with were at the very least moderate drinkers, though most were fairly heavy consumers. Therefore with my background of regular and somewhat heavy alcohol consumption, I perceived I was gaining some higher social status ranking by drinking and keeping up with the best of them. Unfortunately, as mentioned previously, whether through my smaller body mass or not, my tolerance and threshold for how much I could consume before the thin gray line was crossed was significantly lower than most of the people I drank with. My desire was urging me to drink at least as often and as much as my social friends, and in doing so my skewed perception would tell me I was okay and I was just having a good time. Consequently, I would all too regularly cross over that line and regret my behavior later.

There are a limited number of times friends (even less for casual acquaintances) will endure repeated poor behavior from you before their opinion of you is indelibly changed. Hence the reality was my drinking regularly and excessively did not achieve a higher status ranking in the respect and admiration of my social friends and acquaintances, but rather a lower ranking. I now believe that if I wasn't a decent enough, well-liked person and friend to most when I was not drinking, I would have lost a lot of their friendships over those years.

It was like I had two different personas. One was a decent, considerate, polite, respectful, hard-working, and intelligent person, and the other was someone who drank to excess and after crossing over the thin gray line could become depressed, temperamental, insensitive, annoying, sarcastic, and verbally affronting.

After two years of marriage, Donna and I decided to start a family. We had two boys with a two-year gap between them. But unfortunately this didn't stop my regrettable behavior after alcohol-fueled occasions. The birth of our first son was a very difficult one, and after eventually having to have a forced caesarean, Donna had to spend about a week in the hospital to recover. A mate from Hervey Bay and I had already planned a few months in advance to travel back to Monto for our high school's fiftieth year celebration weekend, which now fell a few days after the birth. It was going to be a big event with previous students from the past fifty years coming from near and far to attend. As our baby's delivery was two weeks past the due date, we had expected that Donna and the baby would be well settled back home before this weekend reunion event. As Donna was now going to still be in the hospital over this weekend, she suggested I still go up with my mate to attend.

Now the problem wasn't that I went to the reunion while Donna was still in the hospital with our firstborn child, as she wanted me to go and we both knew she would have lots of friends and family visiting her each day. It was getting so intoxicated in front of many old school friends, parents, and locals I had known from my earlier days growing up in Monto. The mate that I traveled up with is a big bloke and a big drinker. We arrived in town about mid-morning and immediately settled into the local hotel and proceeded to drink and chat with the many locals and friends we knew. I was not only happy to be back chatting with these old friends (and I guess bragging about how I had moved on from this small country town onto bigger and better things), I was also announcing and celebrating the birth of our first son to everyone. We had very little to eat, and by the time the main school reunion parade was about to start, we couldn't be bothered gathering into our school class group to march from the town main street over to the high school. We did drive over to visit the high school briefly for a look though before settling back into the pub.

There was a reunion dance to be held at the shire hall across the road from where we were drinking that evening. However, by the time we decided to go for some dinner at a local restaurant before the dance started, I was well and truly drunk. My memory from the afternoon onward is vague; I remember only bits and pieces. My mate told me I was falling asleep at the restaurant table and was hardly capable of eating any food. My friend was in a better state than I was, so he led me up to the shire hall building where the dance was being held. I should have been taken home to sleep, as I was in no fit state to be in public in front of all these hometown people.

At one stage I remember going outside the hall to where I thought the toilet block was but couldn't find it. I was desperate for a pee and circumnavigated the hall several times looking for the toilets. In the end

I couldn't hold it in any longer and found the nearest bushy shrub and started urinating into it. I did not realize at that time it was situated just outside the main front doors of the hall. Luckily my mate found me at the same time a local policeman did. I am led to believe he was about to take me into custody when my friend said, "He's all right, officer; he's had a bit too much to drink. I'll look after him." The officer indicated that if he didn't get me inside the hall quickly he would charge me. Late that night I did eventually get a lift to my brother's house, where I had arranged to stay. However, the damage to whatever decent image I may have had on leaving Monto years ago was irreparably done.

Early the next morning I was to play golf with a local Monto and ex-college friend, having made the arrangement the day before. I can't remember how I got to the golf course, though I would have only had a few hours' sleep. I recall being still very much affected by alcohol and could not play golf very well at all. The friend I was playing with said he didn't expect me to turn up at all considering the state I was in the night before. By then not only was I starting to feel hungover, I was feeling more and more embarrassed with each memory I recalled and incident that was recounted to me.

To add further to my disgust with myself, we stopped at a local Monto service station café for a light late breakfast after golf. When ordering, the lady greeted me warmly and knowingly, and then asked me how I was feeling. She could tell by my body language that I did not recognize her, so she explained she was the wife of one of my good schoolmates and I had met her the evening before. She also said she thought I may not have remembered her and thought I would be feeling very sick today. All I could do was sincerely apologize for my state the evening before and offer some feeble excuse about not having had any food the day before and trying to keep pace with a seasoned drinker.

On the journey back to Hervey Bay, I became extremely sick from a mixture of severe hangover and car travel sickness. We had to stop a number of times for me to get out and vomit. Instead of that weekend trip being a source of fond memories of meeting and catching up with old friends, teachers, and Monto locals, as well as joyfully celebrating the birth of my son with them, it was one of the worst memories and experiences of drinking too much alcohol that I have. I vaguely remember talking with a few old friends and locals at the dance, though I will never know how many witnessed my grossly intoxicated and shameful state.

With first one then two babies to look after, Donna and I both cut back on the frequency and amount of alcohol we consumed. I must reiterate that prior to her first pregnancy Donna was only a light social drinker anyway and very rarely became unduly intoxicated. She seemed to know when she'd had a sufficient amount on each occasion and would just stop. However, now with the responsibilities of parenthood, she cut back even further.

On the other hand, even though I cut back to take care of my parenthood responsibilities, I still drank too often and too much. It seemed to go in cycles of drinking too frequently and too much, then realizing it was excessive and cutting back for a while. Speaking of cycles, it was at this time (at the start of 1990) that I got involved in triathlons. I started cycling to help strengthen my knee after ligament surgery, and this in turn developed into competing in local and regional triathlons. I was one of the founding members of the Hervey Bay Triathlon Club; I eventually became president, and Donna was secretary for a few years.

After about six years of endless training, I stopped doing triathlons to pursue marathon running, competing in full and half-marathon events around the state. During the eight or so years I was involved in those sports, my alcohol consumption was less frequent due to training commitments, though there were regular binge-type drinking sessions at social events or occasionally alone if having some personal issues.

The frequency may have reduced slightly, though it was if I was playing catch-up when I did drink—a case of all or nothing. It was like I was being so dedicated to years of persistent and grueling training that I felt I had earned the right to get smashed on alcohol once every week or two as a release for built-up stress.

I may have thought triathlons and marathon running were tough endurance training and competition events, though it was alcohol dependency that was my greatest challenge. It was the Himalayas I couldn't cross, my Mount Everest I couldn't climb. I kept getting to base camp, then deciding it was too tough and rationalizing my way back down to the more familiar territory of regular drinking and binge episodes, with excuses like *Every Aussie bloke is expected to drink and occasionally get drunk. All my friends drink and some worse than me. I've been drinking since I was virtually a kid; this is just who I am, and I can't change that.*

Also by this time in my life and marriage, my wife and I weren't going out to public venues socially much anymore. Most of our social life involved friends coming to our house or us going to theirs for dinner parties or to watch football and movies. Perhaps one of the reasons was that we had to be more financially prudent with a house mortgage and raising two children, though I suspect that Donna not trusting me to remain suitably sober may have also been an influence.

Regardless of why we spent more time at home, my alcohol habit adapted to suit drinking at home. At this point, during weekdays I would have my first glass of red wine just before dinner time, and then another with dinner while we watched the news on TV. The kids normally preferred to eat dinner separately while watching their own TV. I more than likely had another wine after dinner and one or two bourbons while we watched other TV shows.

During the weekends it was much the same routine, except the amount of wine or bourbon consumed after dinner was considerably greater while I watched football and then a movie or two after that. During weeknights we would normally go to bed about eight thirty p.m. as standard practice because we had work the next day; however, on weekends it was much later for me and possibly after midnight.

By this time I had usually had so much to drink I had difficulty remembering what I had watched on TV that night. Even though I had a sense that I had enjoyed the footy game, I frequently couldn't remember who won, let alone what the score was. Likewise, if I stayed up late to watch a movie, even though I had a feeling I enjoyed it, I would struggle to remember which movie it was or what had happened in it. As disturbing as this was, I used to sarcastically think to myself, "Oh well, I get to watch the movie again later to see what happens and enjoy it all over again." I do still enjoy watching a really well-made movie with a great script and plot, though in those days it was just as much about having an excuse to stay up drinking as it was to immerse myself in a good movie.

But the worst incidents involving alcohol-corrupted decision making would take me many years to admit to my wife and my sons, and to me they represented the pinnacle of how alcohol was turning me into a person who behaved completely counter to his deepest values and beliefs.

The first incident happened not long before my wife Donna and I started dating. I had broken up with a previous girlfriend several months earlier and was enjoying the extra freedom of being single again. Of course over the years, during the periods of time when I was footloose and fancy-free, my partying and alcohol consumption used to increase significantly. At this particular time, I was working away in another town for a month or so and staying at a hotel during the week. This suited me just fine, as having my room and meals provided in the same building as the licensed bar was ideal. I could come "home" to the hotel from work and drink as much as I liked at the bar, have dinner in the back kitchen, and stagger upstairs to my room at night to sleep. I got to know most of the locals who drank at the hotel and was soon a member of the pub's dart and pool competition teams.

It was during one of these afternoons at the bar I got chatting with a couple of women and became quite friendly with both. One of the women was visiting from out of town and we got on particularly well. We all met up for drinks each night, and they went with our local pub team to neighboring towns on dart or pool competition nights. To this point we had kept our personal details relatively undisclosed, though I suspected the one showing keen interest in me may have had a partner wherever she came from. As I alluded to earlier, just about every evening ended up with me drinking enough alcohol to be fairly intoxicated, so my memory of details of this time nearly thirty years ago are fairly vague. If you consume enough alcohol, all rational judgment goes out the window and you just want to feel good, without thought of any consequences.

So despite my suspecting she may have a partner, one night after a darts night we went back to her place for extra drinks and we ended up having sex. I don't believe I would have made that same decision if I had not been continually loading myself with alcohol every afternoon and evening. I recall in the cold-sober light of day that it didn't feel right, and in hindsight my lifeometer was definitely telling me so. Regardless, my habit of using sex just to feel good, in combination with my alcohol-impaired judgment, saw me acting contrary to my inner ethics.

If you thought having sex with a married woman was a bad enough consequence of my alcohol-affected judgment, the real shock came about nine years later, after I was married. Out of the blue I got a phone call from her. For a while I struggled to place who she was. She informed me she got pregnant that week we were together and I have a child I didn't know about. My head was spinning, as a thousand thoughts were racing through it. I wasn't even sure what I was being told was true, and I told her that if it was, the child has her family and I have mine. That was as the only judgment I could make at the time. Although I told Donna about the phone call about a week after I received it, we decided to mention nothing of this to our boys until they were much older.

As much as I tried to put the knowledge of fathering another child (to a married woman) from my mind and focus on my own family, thoughts of it always managed to pop up on a recurrent basis. In fact, right up until I became alcohol-free, thinking about what had happened and what future unknown events it may lead to was in itself a source for occasions of heavy drinking in a vain attempt to block out those thoughts or just to feel better.

I had learned in no uncertain terms that poor decisions made during alcohol-fueled "good times" can have very serious consequences. What may seem quite reasonable and acceptable when intoxicated can have a lifetime impact on not only our own lives, but also others' lives. The repercussions of that one decision are still being felt nearly thirty years later, as my choice to reveal it in this book as a poignant case of what can happen as a result of alcohol abuse means I have had to now tell my sons about it for the first time. I didn't know what the cost of this revelation to them would be or how much respect I would lose in their eyes. Thankfully, as young adults they were able to see it as the alcohol-related human failing that it was. Hopefully it has encouraged them to give more consideration to their own actions when out partying with friends and to treat alcohol consumption with the acute caution it needs.

The second two incidents (which were even more upsetting for me) happened twenty years ago, when Donna and I were having relationship problems we weren't addressing effectively. We had spent nearly three years being married before planning to have our children, and during that time we were very socially active and attended several parties or social events most weekends. This suited me, as my lifestyle up until being married was just about one big alcohol-driven social event. After so many years of habitually using alcohol to de-stress after work, socialize, and generally feel good, I found it very difficult to change my lifestyle. It was not a matter of not wanting to be a good parent—as I loved my boys more than life itself—however, Donna found it easier to settle into the reduced partying, minimal alcohol maternal role, whereas I continued to drink and socialize at a level much more than I should have.

For a while everything appeared to be changing in a significant way, and I wasn't dealing with it too well. After twenty-six years of one lifestyle (it seemed in only a blink of an eye), I had gone from a relatively self-indulgent, carefree life to the responsibilities and commitments of having one then two baby sons, all the while struggling to change my drinking habit to suit my new circumstances. I had a beautiful, compassionate wife and two gorgeous baby boys whom I loved so much, and I couldn't work out why I felt that wasn't satisfying enough. (I now know I wasn't satisfied because despite having all the external things I wanted, I didn't have the real me. I was not fulfilling my real potential, and because I was a slave to alcohol I was *not* the master of my fate or the captain of my soul. It was *myself* I was unhappy and dissatisfied with.)

Hindsight is indeed a wonderful thing; if only we could have it before the poor decision. Of course this can never be, and in my ignorance my fallback option of alcohol gave me the temporary perception I was feeling good each night I drank (and I did a fair bit every night), though as you can probably predict it only made things worse. As my alcohol consumption increased, our intimacy decreased, and our relationship hit rock bottom. Mind you, we hardly ever argued; we just didn't talk much. You don't have to regularly quarrel to have a poor relationship, and I'm sure many of you have experienced this phenomenon.

At this point I thought our marriage was over. We were virtually living more like friends in the same house rather than like husband and wife. On the surface, though, to all our friends everything would have appeared okay. However, I'm convinced that if we didn't have our two fantastic young boys, whom we both loved with all our hearts, we would have parted ways then. We had even discussed whether that was something we should do; however, we both couldn't bear to cause our boys any pain by separating, so we decided that what we had left of a platonic relationship was better than causing them that heartache. I knew only too well what the gut-wrenching emotional pain caused by divorce was like from my own childhood.

In the depths of this despair, I was in a very dark emotional place and made some decisions that I have regretted ever since. These two particular sins I am guilty of occurred within a week of each other and during the darkest period of our relationship. I had just been offered a new role within my government food standards department. As part of the training provided I had to spend two weeks (all expenses paid) in our state capital city, Brisbane, and then another week in Bundaberg (another city closer to where we lived). This suited me, because given the turmoil of our relationship, I was happy to have some time away. While I was in Brisbane I was mixing with new work colleagues and having copious amounts of alcohol to drink each night at the downtown hotel where I was staying. Life in the big city was more exciting than what I was experiencing at home.

On the last afternoon of the two weeks, I was having quite a few drinks by myself at my hotel's restaurant bar. Later that afternoon a woman sitting next to me and I started chatting. As it turned out, she lived in another Australian state and was in Brisbane on her own for business. We got on well and agreed to have dinner at a nearby hotel where she was staying later that evening. I stayed at my own hotel's bar and kept drinking by myself until it was time to go. To cut a long story short, by the time we met up for dinner, I had had way too many drinks and I suspect she had also. After more drinks over dinner and later at the bar lounge she invited me back to her room. By this time I was very intoxicated and it felt good to have someone intimately desire me.

Although I could still determine going to her room was wrong, my thin gray line had completely dissolved and all rational judgment was gone. (You may recall that it only takes one or two standard drinks [0.01–0.06 percent BAC] before judgment and reasoning are affected, and by five or six drinks [0.11–0.20 percent BAC] all rational judgment is likely gone. I would have consumed more than double that on this occasion.) My marriage was failing, and I just wanted to feel good and, more important, to be desired. Sex and alcohol were my old dependable vices that would surely make me feel better. We did engage in some sexual activity but I was way too drunk to have intercourse. After a short while I said I had better go and staggered back to my own hotel room and passed out.

The next day I had to work and then travel back to Hervey Bay in the afternoon. I was so sick from being hungover that I couldn't eat and was nearly throwing up all morning. I had a nap in my car around lunchtime before very carefully driving the three and a half hours home. I felt so unwell that I could barely focus on my driving, let alone bear to think about what happened the night before. I can vaguely recall feeling a mixture of extreme guilt that I had broken my wedding vow and compromised my internal values with a realization that this was really the end of my marriage. I decided I was not going to tell Donna about my infidelity straight away, but rather take a while to work out how to have the discussion. I was feeling very overwhelmed and distraught, like I was going insane.

Everyone reads stories in tabloids or sees in movies people having too much alcohol at a work Christmas party or a function, and ending up having sex they desperately regret (unfortunately I personally know of a few people where too much alcohol has led to them engaging in non-partner sex). However, we all think it would never happen to us. Well, I'm telling you, if you pour enough alcohol down your throat so your rational judgment is completely shot and your very primal urges to feel good and feel desired are just about the only circuits functioning in your brain, it can and does happen.

The statistics vary greatly depending on the source, though it is reported in the United States alone (with a population of more than 310 million), up to 50–70 percent of relationships experience infidelity, with approximately 30–50 percent of these involving alcohol. It is also reported that 99 percent of people who have cheated hide their infidelity and will deny it when questioned. Less than 1 percent will confess without being confronted, and of those that do, 70–80 percent recover to enjoy stronger marriages in time.[5]

Two days later, after the weekend, I was in Bundaberg for my final week of work training. I was staying at a good motel for the week and it was right next to a local pub. After each day's work I would drive back to my motel and walk next door to the hotel bar to have afternoon drinks. I would stay there drinking until the evening and have some dinner in the open plan dining lounge next to the bar. After eating I would go back to the bar for more drinks before staggering back next door to my motel room to sleep. On one of the last nights I was there, the work colleague training me said he would come to the hotel and join me for dinner. I had my usual lot of afternoon drinks at the bar and a fair few more with my work colleague when he arrived for dinner.

While we were having more drinks at the bar after dinner, he commented that there was a girl who kept "eyeing me off." I didn't pay much attention to it at the time, as we were chatting about what my new work role would be like. It sounded great, as it would give me more autonomy and I would not have to be indoors all the time as in my previous work position.

The night seemed to go quickly, though I guess we were back at the bar for an hour or so after dinner and I had consumed quite a few more drinks. During this time I did notice the girl he had pointed out earlier, as she came up to the bar a few times and smiled at me when ordering her drinks. By the time my colleague left it was quite late and once again I was fairly intoxicated. A short while after he left, the girl came and sat next to me and started chatting. She said she was staying in one of the backpacker-style rooms above the hotel. When I mentioned I was staying in the motel next

---

5   "Adultery: Statistics on Cheating Spouses," December 4, 2009, http://www.examiner.com/article/adultery-statistics-on-cheating-spouses.

door, she asked if my room had a spare bed I was willing to let her sleep in, as she was staying the night in a room with a lot of other backpacker girls who she didn't really like or trust.

Just like the week before, I may have been drunk, but I guessed where this was heading. Even though I was fairly intoxicated (and I had really believed my marriage was all but over), my lifeometer was still trying to tell me this was not a good idea. I'm not sure how many more drinks I had at the bar, though my rational judgment was well and truly gone, and I agreed she could stay in my hotel room. Very regrettably, in my drunken, delusional state of mind, I desperately wanted to feel desired and also consented to her advances of having sex.

The next morning I was severely hungover and suffered enormously all day, not only physically also emotionally. I couldn't believe that despite my significant marriage problems, I had in the space of a week made two monumentally stupid decisions when drunk. They defied everything I felt deep inside: my values, my integrity, my honor, and what little self-worth my alcohol dependency had left me. I had an overwhelming sense I had betrayed Donna, our family, her family, our friends, and everyone who knew me; I had let everyone down. Most of all I felt I had betrayed the "real me" deep inside, the little country boy who just wanted a life of adventure, discovery, and fun. It felt like I had just sold my soul to the devil, and everything I was and stood for was gone.

It was at this point I stopped and really did some serious soul-searching about the path I was on. What were the core things that were really important to me? If I stripped everything else away, what would I most want to have left? This was the type of thing you don't just think about in five minutes. Though the immediate answer to me was family, I spent hours and hours over the next few weeks dedicating deep and authentic thinking about my future and what was important to me and what I should do.

In the end the answer was indeed the love of my family. The more I deeply thought about it, I realized that at my very core I loved both Donna and the boys so much that I would put my life on the line for them; if it came to it, I would die for them if I had to. Furthermore the old and current me would figuratively have to die and be replaced with a better version if I was to salvage and rebuild our relationship into the loving family environment that I really desired. I realized I had to completely let go of my past expectations of a carefree, party lifestyle and focus on what it takes to develop and foster a loving relationship and family environment. This wasn't something I had experienced as a child, and I would need to learn some new skills.

I also realized that I had very little chance of keeping our family together at this low point if I was to reveal my recent immoralities right then, and therefore I chose not to disclose them. Besides, the gravity of what I had done was so heavy and pressing on my moral fiber that I knew I could never again do anything like that in my life (and I haven't). I began to reason, *What possible good could come from telling anyone?* What had happened couldn't be undone, and all the shame, guilt, despair, or penance by me and resentment, anger, desire for revenge, or retribution by Donna would not change it. The revelation would only serve to further harm not only Donna's happiness but also the happiness and well-being of our two boys.

I was not going to let that happen and decided that, as I was the transgressor who violated the expectations of our relationship and marriage, I alone should be the one to bear the emotional consequences of it. To me it seemed completely unjust to unburden my shame and guilt upon Donna in a hope that she would forgive me for what I had done. This would only share my own deep pain and anguish with her and nothing else would change. Even if she forgave me, her forgiveness of me wouldn't change what happened, it wouldn't miraculously make what happened okay, nor would it change how I felt about myself. You can't depend on someone else's permission for you to feel better. That needs to come from inside. The only way I could feel better internally was by coming to terms with what happened, understanding why it happened, looking for what possible good can come from it, finding a way to forgive myself, and changing the way I managed my life from that point forward.

This must have been at the very early stages of the Internet, for I somehow found and purchased an audio and workbook relationship program and some other self-help books. The subject matter I sourced was to do with personal growth and relationships, for as much as I knew I had a problem with alcohol, I still didn't believe for one minute I could ever completely stop drinking. I figured if I could first discreetly learn better relationship and interpersonal skills, I could then manage my alcohol consumption better. I hadn't been brought up in a way that encouraged asking for help or discussing private matters publicly. Therefore, just like I wasn't the type to go to places like Alcoholics Anonymous, I was not going to discuss our private relationship matters with a marriage counselor (though I don't think this was something Donna wanted either). I was determined we could work through our issues on our own and by obtaining materials I could learn from privately.

After I worked through some of these resources myself, I asked Donna if she would do the same, and she did.

As time progressed, our relationship got better. I further developed new skills and understanding from quite a number of different programs and books, including the bestseller *Men Are from Mars, Women Are from Venus* and *Raising Boys*. However, there was still one major thorn in our relationship's side that kept festering up periodically, and that was my alcohol consumption habit. I may have learned and corrected some of the finer points of promoting and maintaining a good intimate relationship and developed better interpersonal skills, though I had not eradicated the number-one cause of virtually every significant self-caused negative impact of my post-childhood life: alcohol. I can without a doubt say that if I had not developed an alcohol habit and subsequent dependency, my life would have been immeasurably better. I would not have been a participant in the inappropriate decisions and activities mentioned earlier in this book, and I would not have been in the position I found myself in during that week of infidelity. You can also be assured any opportunity presented to me to be unfaithful or compromise my values would have been rejected outright. I can't recall one time in my adult life where I have failed in adhering to my values when alcohol wasn't involved.

There were certainly more incidents of significance that I could mention and considerably more of a general embarrassing and regrettable nature, though the intent of this book is not to publicly list every poor and disappointing choice I made while drinking. It is not a full autobiography, rather just a sample of alcohol-related occurrences to give you a feel of how *my* dependency had affected *my* life. I know my friends or acquaintances reading this book could easily add to the list of poor decisions and behavior, though I assure them it is neither necessary nor desired! Though my intent in this book is to focus on the negative aspects of alcohol consumption and how dependent on it people can become, I would like to add that my family and I also had many great times and have many great memories. Without excessive alcohol, I was not normally a person of poor or undesirable character; I strive to live a life of love, compassion, good humor, and sound judgment.

Almost anyone reading my journey to this point could easily be thinking, *For goodness' sake, man—after all that you have seen and done as a result of drinking too much, and now with a wife and young family, why don't you just quit or get help? When sober, don't all these bad consequences motivate you to take some action?*

First, admitting that an alcohol habit is a problem is very, very difficult, no matter how obvious the evidence might be to those around you. Due to pride, the majority of people with alcohol dependencies will never admit it, though they internally feel the full emotional force of the results of their behavior and the perpetual self-deceit. As the stigma of having an alcohol problem is so very personal and humiliating, it is extremely hard to admit it even to yourself, let alone to your friends or publicly. Therefore most of the emotional turmoil is kept inside, creating a raging internal conflict between wanting to be a decent, respectable person and wanting to continue to use alcohol for all the reasons that you currently do—the perceived benefits you think you get.

This internal war that rages can result in you trying to defeat yourself in forms of self-destructive behaviors (including bouts of trying to drink yourself in to oblivion). I suggest that it takes great internal courage especially for men to overcome their pride and to admit that they have an alcohol problem that is now controlling them, rather than the other way around. It is like an admission that they are not strong or manly enough to be able to solve all their problems and take care of everything in their lives. Traditionally men are supposed to be in control and take care of things, so how manly is it going to look if they admit they can't even control their own lives? This is a humiliating and embarrassing admission that most men won't make, even to themselves, unless their emotional manliness and perceived status is somehow preserved. I know I would become quite defensive if my drinking habit was brought into question. I would talk it down and compare my habit to people I knew who were worse in an attempt to make myself feel better and to divert the spotlight from me.

Second, as the next chapter will explain in detail, even when I had admitted to myself that I had a problem and needed to figure out a way to stop, finding the right solution was another problem entirely.

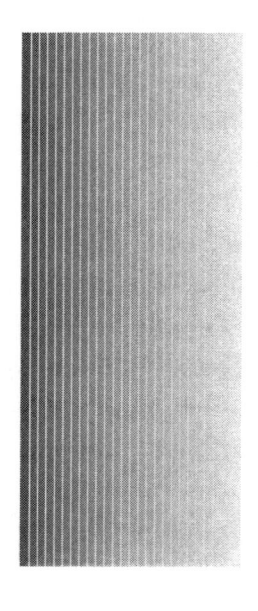

CHAPTER 3

SEARCHING FOR A REMEDY

Although I resisted acknowledging publicly that I had a problem with alcohol, there were moments when I would admit it to myself privately, even in my early twenties. Each unpleasant incident resulting from intoxication would be followed by a period of remorse, and I would say to myself, *This has got to stop. This is not acceptable behavior to me or others. I've got to think out a plan to cut back on how often I drink and set limits on how much each time.* I tried at least two honest approaches to ceasing or controlling my alcohol habit, but because they were both focused on controlling the outward actions rather than getting to the heart level and dealing with my beliefs about alcohol and myself, they were doomed to failure.

My first approach was solely based on my emotions in the moment. From my early twenties on, each feeling of remorse and then resolve would be followed by varying periods of alcohol abstinence, from one day to perhaps a week or two. I remember once even begrudgingly stopping for a month, though never really considered stopping altogether. Usually after the initial emotional pain and embarrassment of the triggering event started to fade away and I had felt that a suitable period of penance had passed, I would again turn to my habitual behavior of using alcohol.

Naturally I wouldn't need much of an excuse to resume. It could be just to help me relax or deal with stress, to celebrate some trivial event, or just that it was socially expected in certain circumstances. Of course I would convince myself that I would only have one or two drinks just to take the edge off that stressful day or issue. Or just have a couple drinks to be part of celebrating that happy occasion. Though once the gate was opened it wouldn't take long to be back to my regular drinking habits.

You see, I firmly believed alcohol was the accepted (and possibly the only real) tool to use in these situations. Non-drinkers might use medication, food, or other tools and techniques less harmful than alcohol or drugs to help manage life's highs and lows; however, that is not who I was. I had myself convinced that as I was born and bred in a tough country environment, a real man's coping tool of choice had to be alcohol. I just needed to figure out a way to not step over that thin gray line between being in control and behaving badly—well, not too far over, anyway—and if I did, not too often, anyway.

The Moment of Choice

My alcohol habit has been devastating enough even if I take an entirely personal (and somewhat selfish) view on how it affected just my own life and health, without factoring in other people. Certainly alcohol has caused many unnecessary problems in my life and has undeniably limited who I could have become and what I could have accomplished. I allowed my alcohol habit to mask the true nature of who I really was and desired to become. That was the tragic reality for far too many years and should be reason enough for people reading this to closely examine their own lives.

However, even more painful and disappointing is the effect my habit has had on people I have loved, do love, or care deeply about. My immediate family had endured too many embarrassing moments and witnessed or heard too many stories of unacceptable behavior. I wasn't as fully engaged with them or available to them as I could have been if I was alcohol-free. But even worse, not only was my habit now creating issues for them, I was also (by way of example) condoning the excessive use of alcohol as common practice to my two boys. This became unacceptable to me (especially as a parent), and further motivated me to permanently cease.

I remember when my boys quietly approached me one afternoon and asked if they could have a chat with me. I could see the tentative looks on their young faces and hear the nervousness in their voice as they said they had some friends coming over to play and for a sleepover that night. They went on to ask could I please not have too much to drink when they were here. Furthermore, if I was having my usual drinks, could I please not go out into the games room to talk with them. When I asked what the matter was, they went on to say they were very embarrassed about me slurring my words, making jokes that weren't funny, and generally "geeing them up" as a bit of fun. They said their friends would have a laugh about me when I left the room.

I was shattered. Here I was, their father, who should have been their idol and mentor, someone they should look up to, admire, and be proud of, being told I was an embarrassment to them and their good friends. Up to that point in time, I might have presented myself to them after a few too many drinks occasionally over that last year, but I was not aware my behavior was at all embarrassing. I had thought I was genuinely witty and funny (as we all do after drinking alcohol). This was the first time they had built up the courage to approach me, with what would have been a very uncomfortable subject for them to raise. Although Donna had quietly told me a few times over the last few years that the boys had expressed concerns they thought I drank too much occasionally, I didn't realize they were actually ashamed of my behavior. I felt like my heart had been ripped out and I had lost their love. I could make excuses for myself and cope with my own lack of great success in life, though my intrinsic compulsion to do the best I could for my family could not be compromised or excused away. I was not behaving in a way congruent with whom I knew I truly was inside, and I had to change my behavior. I had to find a way to turn it around, cease drinking, and end my habit.

Additionally, many good friends and some colleagues and acquaintances over the years had made derogatory comments about my alcohol consumption or my behavior resulting from it. I knew what type of person I was deep down, and to know that I repeatedly contradicted those standards in front of my friends or colleagues while intoxicated caused me great embarrassment, internal conflict, and stress. It eventually got to the stage where I was so paranoid about drinking too much and behaving badly that I disliked and resisted going out to functions with friends, preferring to drink at home or in places where no one knew me. I didn't respect myself because of my alcohol habit, so why should anyone else? The only time I felt relaxed was when I was by myself, and even then there were times I was not comfortable in my own skin because of my drinking. That is not a good state to be in.

An epic internal struggle warred inside me, seemingly between good and evil, and not unlike a Jekyll and Hyde personality. In fact, occasionally friends had mockingly commented, "your evil twin made an appearance last night." I knew how good the real me was, and yet after too much alcohol (even if seemed like just a few drinks), I would morph into a seemingly a different personality, often embarrassing myself and those that cared about me. The next day I would emotionally die a thousand deaths, realizing I had behaved in a way that was yet again contrary to my values and behavioral expectations.

Soon there wasn't a day that went by that I didn't worry about my dependency and the embarrassing effects it could have on me and others. Every day I had to be on guard against drinking too much. This inner conflict was so emotionally draining that something would have to give. It is now known that this type of stress or "dis-ease" is the catalyst for physical diseases and cancers.

There comes a time when hard decisions have to be made, and I knew I had to make a choice, not just for the sake of my family or my friends, but for me. I wanted to be all I knew I could be, the real me. The me who once loved to ride and trek the hills, valleys, dense scrub, and open grazing land.

The me who would think great thoughts and imagine great adventures of travel and discovery. The me who felt stress-free and didn't have this sinister cloud constantly looming over me, waiting for the next storm and direct lightning strike.

The Failure of Behavior Management Alone

My first determined attempt of actually doing something about the frequency and amount I was drinking was nearly fifteen years after Donna and I were married. I knew I had to earnestly do something about my drinking, though I wasn't sure what. My plan of monitoring my habit and trying to keep it in check wasn't working. Attempting to use my willpower to curb the amount I drank wasn't enough. As a competitive athlete and analytical thinker, I generally have strong determination and willpower to achieve things I desire. But I just couldn't seem to get good results applying my willpower to this habit.

Recognizing this, I even asked a doctor to prescribe some tablets that were supposed to reduce the chemical reward response in the brain. However, I was too embarrassed to admit I had an alcohol dependency to my own doctor, as he was also an old cricket teammate. Instead, I asked for the prescription when I was getting a routine skin cancer check done by a local GP specialist whom I didn't know personally. Anyway, these tablets didn't do any good in reducing my desire for alcohol.

After some heart-to-heart discussions with my wife, I wanted to demonstrate to her (and myself) that I was prepared to put some steadfast structure around my drinking habits. It didn't take too much analysis to determine that it was both the *frequency* with which I was consuming alcohol and the *amount* I consumed each time that were a concern, although on the surface it did seem that the major problem was *how much* I drank each time. One or two drinks was never enough; I wasn't satisfied unless I was feeling the warm, pleasant buzz from becoming intoxicated (a sense of feeling good). I'm sure all of you with alcohol habits of your own can relate to that feeling where after a certain number of drinks you are feeling relaxed and all your cares seem to dissolve away. I couldn't see the point in drinking unless I could get a decent buzz or sense of euphoria from the session. If I had to stop after just one or two drinks, I felt I was being robbed of my goal and at times could get quite disappointed.

Depending on individual factors (such as genetics, rate of consumption, tolerance, and gender), the average person's body can eliminate the alcohol from approximately one standard drink in about an hour. Therefore, except for the psychological dependency and perhaps financial implications stemming from consuming small amounts of alcohol on a frequent basis, someone who regularly drank only a few drinks at a rate of no more than one standard drink per hour is not likely to suffer any acute behavioral problems resulting from intoxication. For me, however, I wanted to address the *amount* I consumed each time as the primary cause of my *behavioral* issues and also address the *frequency* with which I drank as the *dependency* issue, because I was drinking every single night.

So I experimented with implementing a few different personal rules designed to address the two concerns identified. The first was to limit drinking alcohol only to the weekends, and I defined the weekend as Friday night through to and including Sunday night: a four-day-off, three-day-on system. This didn't work too well, because I felt like I was fighting against my totally entrenched habit during the weekdays, and then had the urge to make up for lost drinking time on Friday night (watching sports or movies) and over the rest of the weekend. On Sunday afternoon and evening I knew I wouldn't be having any alcohol until the following Friday night, so I would tend to have a generous session then as well. My weekday consumption was nil, while my weekend consumption seemed to increase; therefore the behavioral aspects on the weekends did not improve. As many of you will know, to support the existence of our alcohol habits we become very good at trying to disguise how much we have actually drank and how intoxicated we really are. We make a conscious effort to think, talk, and act as normally as possible. Clearly this can last only until the obvious and unavoidable physical telltale signs start to show. When I used to witness those vain attempts by others at acting sober, I used to think it was rather comical; now I think it is quite sad.

One of my next attempts at a solution was to deal with the excess amount consumed on the weekends, as well as the sense of deprivation

I felt during the weekdays. You should understand by now my use of alcohol to relax from any stresses at work or life in general was an entrenched habitual behavior for me. Hence any forced attempt to change this would be mentally resisted and have psychological and brain chemical consequences. So this new plan involved cutting back to just two glasses of wine around dinner time each week night and no more than two glasses of bourbon extra on Friday and Saturday nights only. Although this still felt like an unwelcome restriction to me, it seemed like an affirmative action that I could reluctantly manage. It would allow me to have a few drinks each night (like I was used to) and *only* a couple more on the weekends, without any of the negative behavioral occurrences previously experienced. As I had not reached the desire to stop consuming alcohol completely—nor did I believe I ever could stop drinking completely—this plan of setting fixed drink limits appeared to be the best alternative.

Over the next few years this plan did have the desired effect on the primary issue of drinking too much on any one occasion. I wasn't perfect, and on the odd occasion I would go over my weekend limits—though overall it seemed to work okay. There were times when either Donna or I were away on business or for the weekend and I would deliberately drink more, seeking that sense of totally relaxed, careless abandon. However, on the whole it drastically reduced alcohol-related incidents to near nil and yet was appeasing my desire to continue drinking. Though I was still drinking alcohol every night, because of the reduced amounts at each session I noticed the benefits from it—simple things like a renewed vigor and enthusiasm to get up very early on Saturday mornings and play golf with my mates in the local club competition, whereas previously this was becoming rarer due to me feeling hung-over and thus playing poorly.

During this time of my limiting alcohol plan, I also experimented with things like making my own lower-alcohol drinks and therefore increasing the volume I could drink. At times I would mix full-strength red wine with nonalcoholic red wine, reducing the overall alcohol percentage by one half. I even got some pure distilled alcohol off a friend of a friend and added precise percentages of this to bottles of alcohol-free wine to make my own low-alcohol blend. I similarly lowered the alcohol content of my spirits drinks by either halving the amount of spirit I put in a glass with the soft drink mix, or increasing the size of the glass and also the mixer.

You should understand that my habit was such that I was used to drinking at home every night, and it didn't feel normal to have dinner or sit watching television without an alcoholic drink to sip on. I reasoned that by having lower alcohol content drinks, I could still have most of the flavor and perceive I was consuming as much alcohol as before (even though I wasn't). What I discovered, though, was that I ended up drinking my drinks at a quicker pace and usually consumed about twice as much. At best this plan was just another ineffective temporary management strategy that did not do anything to address *why* I felt the need to routinely drink alcohol at all.

Because I was aware of the problem and I was working on a plan, I convinced myself I was proactively addressing the problem. In reality both approaches described above—whether I attempted to control the amount of alcohol I consumed in the moment, or planned ahead of time what my limits would be—were simply external management and damage control strategies and were doomed to fail. Why? I believed I was someone who would *always* use alcohol socially and as a therapeutic remedy. Hence this left a very small area to focus on: how often and how much I was going to drink. This kind of external strategy didn't consider my mindset or beliefs at all. It didn't consider the whole picture of *why* I was drinking, let alone why I was drinking too much. It didn't consider what I perceived I was getting out of alcohol versus how I could get that benefit in another way. It didn't take into account what my true inner values and beliefs were, and if they had ever been compromised or mutated by outside influences during my life.

I also believed that consuming alcohol was an important part of my Australian identity. My belief was that, as a fair dinkum Australian male, I was expected to drink alcohol, certainly at all social occasions. To do the contrary would be considered downright un-Australian and less manly.

In other words, I was so convinced in my mind that, given my upbringing and history, drinking alcohol was now an intrinsic part of me. I vehemently believed that being a regular consumer of alcohol was a part of who I was and my station in life. I did not see myself ever being a non-drinker of alcohol. That seemed a total impossibility to me, and I emphatically believed it would never happen. I distinctly remember having a particular conversation with Donna concerning my drinking habits where I stated exactly that to her. I told her that I did not see myself ever being a non-drinker and the best she and I could expect was that I would manage the frequency and amount I drank to a tolerable level. Inwardly I had determined that if I could just monitor and manage the progression of my alcohol habit, I may make it to a reasonable old age before dying—that is, make it through life without ending up like the old stereotypical alcoholic you see on television, perhaps homeless and drinking out of a bottle in a brown paper bag. It is extremely sad to think that for a period of time I had resigned myself to the thought my life was going to be lived and controlled by my alcohol habit.

In truth, this solemn belief that drinking alcohol was a now a core part of me was preventing any chance of me breaking the habit. We always produce results aligned to our primary beliefs and thoughts. I now know I would have never succeeded in even properly *managing* my alcohol consumption, let alone stopping it altogether, if I had kept that belief. As you will read later, changing that belief was the key that opened the door to the solution.

So the inner war raged on between (a) wanting to continue to get the perceived benefits from drinking and not suffer the social rejections and alienation of being a non-drinker, and (b) logically seeing the real benefits to my health, close personal relationships, work, sports, and even finances if alcohol was not a part of my life. The inner conflict also battled between (a) believing that drinking alcohol was so firmly entrenched in my psyche and body that I would always be a drinker until the day I died, and hence resigned to managing the consumption, and (b) knowing I was a sound, intelligent, logical, and analytical thinker with good core values who also wanted more out of life and believed I was the master of my own destiny. Some of these desires and beliefs seem paradoxical in nature, and there lies a key to the problem and the solution. I needed to resolve how on one hand

I believed I was locked in to being a drinker all my life, and on the other I believed I had the personal power to determine my own future.

The Turning Point: Examining Inward Reasons

In giving this much deeper thought, I came upon the key that would eventually set me on the road to success. I began to look inward at my beliefs and reasons for drinking, rather than focusing on my outward actions and controlling my behavior through willpower alone. I determined I needed to examine exactly what my core beliefs were and analyze whether they were still valid for me at this point in my life. *Why* did I believe I needed to drink alcohol, and *why* did I believe I couldn't live without it? What was I really trying to achieve by drinking, and could I achieve that another, healthier way?

I also had to give some serious thought to what I really desired and wanted out of life for me personally. Not what I thought others wanted for me or what current traditions or society may seem to mandate is expected of me—simply what do I want at a core level. What makes me genuinely and naturally feel good at my center, not just superficially? To determine this I would have to reflect on my basic core values, the qualities of thought and behavior that I wished to personally uphold and that I also valued in other people. I needed to start with this foundation of internal values and review and examine my specific beliefs with these values. From there I could review and examine my actions stemming from my beliefs to determine whether they are also aligned with my values. I needed to review and change *who* I was before I could ever change *what* I did. I realized I had to cut through and set aside the cultural, manly, and learned beliefs I had adopted and examine what I really felt and desired deep inside. I had to temporarily become more self-centered to determine what I really wanted before I could become more selfless and valuable to others.

I propose that people develop most of their substance dependencies or habits in an attempt either to gain some pleasure and excitement that is lacking in their life or to suppress negative experiences—or both, depending on the circumstances of their upbringing and current situation. I also submit that the people with the most severe negative habits (or greatest number of them) are people who don't feel good about themselves and are trying to feel better by blocking or replacing emotional pain. They are drawn to and tend to sustain habits like alcohol, drugs, obsessive compulsive eating, sex, or even attitudes like perpetually finding fault in everyone else in an attempt to make themselves feel better than they do. I know that I have been guilty of using all these to varying degrees in an effort to feel better. People with a higher degree of self-love, self-respect, and contentment are more likely to have no attraction to negative habits designed to make themselves feel better. The secret is to educate yourself, change your beliefs and thinking, and then act in ways that generate higher self-esteem and inner satisfaction. Only in this way can you eliminate the need for external vices and habits that serve as surrogates for true internal happiness. Reading and listening to inspiring personal development material is essential to shifting your inner beliefs and thoughts to ones that support your success.

I decided that only by following my *internal* review process could I hope to change my *externally* manifested habit of alcohol consumption with any real conviction. I knew the key element was to complete the mental resolution process of my dependency before even starting to deal with the physical part of the habit. I came to realize that I was letting my past and present circumstances govern my thoughts, feelings, and actions. The more I focused my mind on what I perceived was negative in my life, the more I attracted circumstances to feel negative about. I had to turn this around to have new thoughts and feelings drive new, success-enhancing actions, which would in turn result in better personal circumstances. I had been using a natural universal law of "we attract what we predominantly think about" to my detriment, by dwelling my mind on things I didn't want.

On the physical resolution side of my habit, I also realized from additional research material I had studied[6] that there would be some physical reaction to the sudden and sustained absence of the main chemical in alcoholic beverages, ethyl alcohol, also known as ethanol. As an adaptation to the presence of alcohol in the bloodstream, the brain responds by increasing or inhibiting the function of some important neurotransmitters, particularly

---

6 A list of the personal developmental material I studied during this time can be found at www.alcohemy.com.

glutamate (excitatory), GABA (inhibitory), dopamine (reward/pleasure), and serotonin (mood/feeling). In very simplified terms, if you suddenly stop your habitual alcohol intake, your adapted brain misses the artificially induced dopamine/GABA levels usually triggered by ethanol, and you experience symptoms of withdrawal.

When people stop taking alcohol or drugs that have this effect on their brain, there is a period of time when their body has to adjust to regulating its own levels of neurotransmitters. The amount and the longevity of these symptoms depend on the frequency and amount of alcohol the person used to consume. These adaptations the brain has put in place may be very minor and temporary in a person new to consuming alcohol who only drinks occasionally, whereas they can be significant adaptations and become more fixed for someone who consumes large amounts of alcohol frequently. Some of these brain changes were revealed in Pavlov's dog experiment in the 1890s, where physiologist Ivan Pavlov noted a dog's biochemical and physical responses to the expectation of receiving food. In the case of alcohol, if it is consumed regularly and activates certain brain reward and sedation responses (by affecting dopamine and GABA levels) in a way that makes us feel good, we are similarly conditioned to drink alcohol when we want to feel good.

To illustrate this point, ask yourself if you can easily go thirty days without feeling like you need to have an alcoholic drink. If your answer is no, you have developed either a psychological or physical dependency on alcohol (or, more likely, both).

If we regularly drank in certain environments, and/or with certain people, and/or at certain times, and/or with certain foods, and so on, we could develop strong associations with those conditions to drinking alcohol and feeling good. If you encounter those same conditions or environment when abstaining from alcohol, the previously established associations would be telling your brain to expect some ethanol to feel good, and in its absence cravings plus withdrawal symptoms can be triggered.[7] To add to

---

7   National Institute on Alcohol Abuse and Alcoholism, *Alcohol Alert* no. 54, October 2001, http://pubs.niaaa.nih.gov/publications/aa54.htm; Linda Ray, "How Long Does Alcohol Withdrawal Last?" eHow Health, http://www.ehow.com/about_5081312_long-alcohol-

the mix, in heavy drinkers the cognitive and prefrontal cortex part of the brain, where reasoning, judgments, and decisions are made, often becomes compromised during habitual drinking and for some time after abstaining. This reduces the mental ability to appropriately override these cravings by rationalizing the benefits of abstaining. With a compromised cognitive/reasoning capacity, the desire to temporarily feel good can override rational judgment, and alcohol consumption relapses can occur.

The Missing Ingredient: Belief

Up until around this time, even though I had been rekindling my interest in personal advancement educational material and was focused on my inward reality rather than outward behavior as the key to change, I still wasn't convinced I could overcome this particular deep-seated habit. Having the belief I could do it was also going to be a *very* important component for me to be successful. I want to emphasize that believing it *could* be done was different from the belief that *I* could do it.

My logical mind already knew it *could* be done, as I was aware that other people around the world with serious alcohol dependencies did stop drinking. However I did not personally know any I could ask how they went about it. The extent of my knowledge until then from reading and TV programs was that people had great difficulty and usually attended Alcoholics Anonymous meetings for years in a battle against the "demon" alcohol. As I mentioned previously, whether through pride, embarrassment, stubbornness, or the refusal to be officially labeled an alcoholic, I was not going to even contemplate going to those type of meetings for help.

Furthermore, I didn't want to be in a constant battle and fighting the urge to drink for years to come. Some dated (1990) though worrying statistics I found indicated that one-quarter (26 percent) of those who first attend an AA meeting still attended after one year. Furthermore, nearly one-third (31.5 percent) left the program after one month, and by the end of the third month, almost half (47.4 percent) left. Of those who stay for three months, half (50.0 percent) will attain one year of sobriety. Another

---

withdrawal-last.html; Roger (no last name given), "Alcohol—How Food Can Reduce Cravings," Wild Health, http://www.wildhealthfood.com/how-food-can-reduce-alcohol-cravings.

North American survey showed after coming to AA, 65 percent received outside treatment or counseling, and 84 percent of those members said that outside help played an important part in their recovery.[8]

This confirmed to me the secret I finally discovered, which was that you can have all the well-intentioned moral support in the world, but if you don't have and use the psychological tools to change your thoughts and beliefs internally, nothing will change permanently on the outside. You may see some temporary change through sheer determination and "gutsing it out," though as soon as your support is absent, your inner core desire will coax you back to drinking. This is what I was referring to earlier when I said I didn't want to spend the rest of my life fighting the urge to have a drink. I wanted to not just be physically alcohol-free; I wanted to be totally and permanently psychologically free from alcohol as well.

My intensified studying of material on increasing human potential was most certainly a key ingredient in me gaining the belief that I could break this habit and overcome my dependency. Over several years I read many books and listened to many recordings of this type of material, which helped in all areas of my life. There was one story in particular that may well have been the tipping point in my belief I would succeed. It made such an impact on me because it provided scientific evidence that if I follow a particular set of different actions for a set period of time, those new actions will become normal to me, or become a new habit. I originally heard this story in Bob Proctor's recordings, and then researched it myself. In this recording, he describes an experiment that NASA conducted during early space travel times. They wanted to see how astronauts would cope with zero gravity and the disorientation from not readily knowing up from down. They had the test subjects wear special goggles twenty-four hours a day that inverted everything they could see, so that everything appeared upside down. They could not take these goggles off at all, even while showering or in bed. As you would expect, there were significant physical and emotional symptoms of disorientation,

---

8 *Comments on AA Triennial Surveys*, Alcoholics Anonymous World Services, December 1990. Referenced in "Alcoholics Anonymous," Wikipedia, http://en.wikipedia.org/wiki/Alcoholics_Anonymous.

as the brain failed to make sense of these new visual signals, given the reality was opposite to what they were seeing.

However, somewhere between the twenty-six day and the thirtieth day, to everyone's amazement, an unexpected phenomenon took place. The test subjects started to see everything the correct way up again. The brain had adapted by rewiring the way it interpreted the visual signals to make what they were seeing look normal as compared to the reality they had always known.

They repeated the experiment and got some subjects to take their goggles off for one day at various points up to day twenty-six. What they noted was that these subjects had to have the goggles back on for an additional twenty-six to thirty days before their vision swapped to the right way up. Hence it had to be twenty-six to thirty consecutive days before the brain confirmed the change was necessary and completed the required rewiring. Furthermore, once the brain had switched to suit the goggles, when the test subjects removed them, what they saw appeared upside down again, as the artificially inverted signals had become normal to them. After the goggles were removed, it took another twenty-six to thirty days for the brain to correct the vision to the correct way up again.

This indicated to me that the brain would adapt to any new stimulus or routine and program itself to treat it as the new normal, provided that new stimulus or routine was continued daily (without disruption) for at least thirty consecutive days. Though this new belief was just one element of the process, I now had something tangible I could set a psychological and physical plan around. I wouldn't have to guess and wonder about how long it would take (if it happened at all). I now had hope that fighting alcohol would not have to be a lifelong battle of feeling constant cravings and fighting against a habit that I couldn't break. Now I had a belief *I* could break the habit permanently, strengthened by scientific research—conducted by NASA, at that. All it required now was a strategy to get me from day one to day thirty.

I was fairly confident of achieving that—after all, I had done it at least once before. The difference was that back then it was typically an act of doing harsh penance after a particularly shameful alcohol-related incident, and I had every intention of drinking again after that time was up. I figured it would be a bit easier this time now I could see light at the end of the tunnel, as opposed to not knowing how long the tunnel was or what it would be like at the end of it. Doing something with a known ending is not that brave. Risking yourself with an unknown outcome is scary and takes courage.

Even though my overall plan was to stop drinking indefinitely, my immediate more believable plan was to go thirty days and see what needed to be adjusted then. It was a lot like Thomas Carlyle's famous quote: "Go as far as you can see; when you get there, you'll be able to see farther." I planned to break it down into small manageable weekly pieces (which seemed achievable), and as I added each next small piece on, it too would seem manageable. Additionally, I would need to create and implement a daily plan that would cover each particular facet of my current alcohol-related habitual behavior during the week.

As you can see, a multipronged approach was required to give me the best chance of a permanent solution to both the emotional and the physical components of my alcohol dependency habit. You may have noticed I sometimes use the words "dependency" and "habit" together and sometimes individually. I do this because, regarding alcohol addiction, I believe they go hand in hand. I became dependent on alcohol consumption because from a very early age I started forming a habit of using it to feel better. Likewise, the more I became dependent on the chemical to feel better, the more entrenched my habit of using it became. Now I wanted to break my habit of drinking alcohol to become independent of the effects of ethanol on my brain and body.

I came to realize that, after all, the human body and mind were not designed with ethyl alcohol as a necessary nutrient. In fact, to our body it is a poison that causes intoxication, and the body reacts by trying to eliminate as much of it as possible as quickly as possible. The reality was that I had a habit of chronically poisoning myself each and every day. Humans were meant to use our bodies and minds in our natural states to experience happiness and sadness, pleasure and pain, stress and relaxation, so we can learn what we like and dislike and develop natural health strategies to manage them.

The Three Key Ingredients: Why, How, and Belief

Once I had made the firm decision to stop drinking, it was actually a bit exciting. It almost felt like I was starting out on a voyage of discovery, going into unchartered seas or setting out on a journey across some unknown wasteland, not sure what perils or treasures lay ahead—a bit like when I was a young boy back on the property at Monto, fantasizing about far-off adventures. This adventure was very real, though, and not only tinged with excitement but also quite frightening. This wasn't the fear of immediate physical danger associated with something like climbing Mount Everest; nonetheless, my long-term physical and emotional health, as well as the future of my closest relationships, would depend on a safe and successful completion of this journey to becoming alcohol-free.

I believe the primary keys to my success were the five points listed below. I was willing to spend quality time really thinking about the first four points, and then taking the fifth but crucial step of formulating an action plan:

1. Looking back over the whole of my life, how did my alcohol dependency develop? Why had I wanted to start drinking, and why did I now want to stop?
2. What perceived benefits versus harm did I believe resulted from me drinking, and how did these relate to my core values?
3. What fears did I have about not only stopping altogether, but also even attempting to try to stop?
4. How could I reinforce the belief that I could actually stop drinking, and what mental tools and strategies could help me?

And then, the final step:

5. Formulate a plan, thought out in advance, on how to start, progress, and cope with issues that would surely arise.

Now when I say I was "really thinking about" these points, I don't mean I gave them a superficial once-over or a quick jog down memory lane. I mean deep, authentic thinking, where I looked at not only *what* happened, but also *why* it happened and *how* I was feeling at that time. Not only *what* my beliefs were, but also *why* I believed them and *where* those beliefs came from. Only by being willing to spend time at that deep level of thought was I able to clarify where I had come from, where I currently was, and where I needed to change to succeed. These mental contemplations of my past and present did not happen overnight, and at times it was not emotionally easy or convenient. I did not get to the alcohol dependency condition I was in overnight, and it wasn't going to be resolved overnight. Regardless of whether it takes you a few days or a few weeks, it is important to be thorough and honest if you really want to make permanent changes to your life. This isn't a "just add water and stir" remedy.

As you will see from the list above and the Alcohemy process that follows, the mental preparation element (determining the why and the belief) was just part of the process. I then had to develop the how: a plan to journey forward day by day and week by week. This plan had to address all the changes to be made and the obstacles I was likely to encounter. Of course, as in any major endeavor, there were indeed some challenges along the way, but I have to say that, because of the process and planning I had already completed before starting, it was not as bad as I had expected.

In summary, the approach outlined by the five items listed above can be condensed to three key elements: *why*, *how*, and *belief*. All three are interlinked and support each other. The *why* consisted of two parts: (1) why I started and formed my habit, plus (2) why I wanted to stop. The *how* was an end-to-end process I could follow that would not only systematically examine the why elements, but it would give me a step-by-step plan to follow so I wouldn't be second-guessing what to do next. The *belief* I needed was the specific belief that I could actually do it (not just that it was technically possible) and see it through to completion.

Once Again, the Captain of My Soul

As time progressed from the first day of abstaining, it actually got easier and the satisfaction and sense of accomplishment I felt added to my resolve. I gained forward momentum with each milestone passed. I had already prepared for most obstacles I encountered, so they were no match for my new mindset that I did not need to use alcohol for any reason whatsoever. I was again becoming master of my own mind.

As stated in the introduction, the poem titled "Invictus" by William Ernest Henley really resonated with me during this process, and I used to say the last verse in my mind when I had any challenges. I have added the last verse again here, as I found it just so powerful, and I hope it inspires you as well.

> *It matters not how strait the gate,*
> *How charged with punishments the scroll.*
> *I am the master of my fate:*
> *I am the captain of my soul.*

I truly felt I was again the captain of my soul, rather than habitually making poor (sometimes irrational) decisions and behavior choices when I inevitably crossed the thin gray line. My habit was like a very dark and ominous cloud of impeding trouble that was always hovering and rumbling over my head, and I never knew when and where the lightning would strike next. Previously the stress of knowing that at some point in the future I would slip up and create an embarrassing and regrettable moment was always with me. It was an ever present, nagging, gnawing feeling in my mind and the pit of my stomach, especially if we were going out to dinner or some social occasion. Now this cloud had disappeared, and I had absolutely no care in the world that I would ever have any alcohol-related issues again.

I can't emphasize enough how much of a difference being alcohol-free has made in my life. Usually when asked about the best thing you've ever done in your life, most people will say either marrying/partnering with their loved one or having their children. Yes, while these are certainly my top events, becoming alcohol-free is a very strong contender. It certainly is the single most important personal improvement I have made in my lifetime.

The confidence I have now regained when going out to group social occasions is simply a reward just in itself. Whereas I used to use alcohol as an aid to give me false confidence, now I go out to any occasion knowing everything I do and say is completely the real me for the entire day or evening.

Also, before I quit alcohol, most often Donna would stay under the driving alcohol limit, or we would get a taxi to local social events, as I always drank beyond the driving limit. Now I take pride in always being able to drive and quite readily offer to drive friends to and from social events also if they wish. I quite enjoy driving the minibus when my golfing mates and I travel away to play other golf courses, as most of them have quite a few drinks during and after these social rounds of golf. Previously I would have been one of the group getting intoxicated at the end of the day.

My personal relationships with my wife and my sons have also improved as a result of my alcohol-free lifestyle. Donna had always been perplexed as to why I would constantly drink to excess. She said she knew the type of person I was when I was sober: intelligent, analytical, always passionate about doing the right thing, creating a good impression, and being an example to others. She said she couldn't understand how I would put myself in the situation where I was behaving virtually the opposite of the values she knew I embraced. Thus it was a great relief to her to have the person she knew and loved in a normal and true state of mind 100 percent of the time.

Not only was this return to our appreciation of each other as our true selves a boost to our relationship as best friends, but likewise our intimacy was enriched to levels beyond what we had experienced for some years. Let's face it: most of us would rather be intimate with our partner when he or she is in a natural state and unaffected by alcohol. As I was having at least a few drinks every night, she didn't get to experience me like that.

We also resumed going for long early morning exercise walks on the weekends, and then having breakfast afterward at one of the beachside cafés. We started going to the local cinema to watch a movie together most weekends. Occasionally I would drive us to evening dinners at local restaurants, now with us both being completely at ease, knowing the evening would not be affected by any alcohol-related concerns. The previous constant degree of tension waiting for the next incident was now gone and replaced by a very much appreciated atmosphere of relaxed enjoyment.

I was also now a more complete role model for my teenage sons, without the stigma of being a parent who drank too much hanging over our relationship. Now that I didn't drink or smoke, I developed a stronger relationship with them, plus I promoted and lived according to other decent values. I was finally able to set the kind of example that I always wanted to set for my boys.

Even though we never discussed the subject until several years after I stopped drinking, I knew straightaway that my boys felt a relief that neither they nor their visiting friends would ever have to see me in an intoxicated state again. Also, during their younger years, if my sons ever needed a lift to an event or a friend's place in the evenings, Donna would usually have to be the one to drive them, as I would have had a few drinks by then. I actually remember selfishly thinking on a few occasions, "Why couldn't people plan their activities better, given that they know I have drinks in the evening?" In fact, if anything at all affected my ability to have my routine evening drinks, I would be very annoyed. Since becoming alcohol-free, I have gladly played the role of chauffeur to the boys and Donna whenever needed and see it as an opportunity to help the people I care about.

Ceasing alcohol has also paid dividends for the work that I did as a staff supervisor for the electrical distribution company. I became crystal-clearheaded and vibrant every morning. Even though over the last few years before I stopped drinking I was "only" having no more than two glasses of wine on weeknights, my clarity of mind and thought was not as good as it became once I was alcohol-free. I believe this had more to do with the consistent, chronic nature of my alcohol consumption rather than how much I was drinking each night. Having no alcohol in my system for years now has given me a clarity of perception, reasoning, and judgment I had never experienced before. Every day I arrive at work full of vigor and have the enthusiasm and stamina to cope with the most demanding days.

Financially, no longer consuming alcohol has been a major expense saving. Even when I was only having my two glasses of red wine on weeknights, I was spending about A$90 per week, or A$4,700 per year, on just the alcohol I drank at home. This was purely my expense, as Donna never drank at home unless there was a social occasion when guests were also drinking. Due to our reasonable combined incomes, I chose to drink quality red wine and bourbon with some top-end cask red wine for backup. Of course when we went out on weekends it was more expensive to drink at hotels and clubs, so this would have added to the overall alcohol expense quite a bit. Donna had relatively few drinks when we went out socially, though it would be usual for the combined alcohol expense alone to be close to A$100.

If I added to this the associated expenses that went with a night out for drinks at a hotel or club, like playing the poker machines and keno, then it would be quite a bit more money. Often the decision on how much to gamble on the poker machines and when to stop became corrupted by the effect of the amount of alcohol consumed, resulting in spending a lot more than originally anticipated.

After I went through the psychological Alcohemy process I developed to stop drinking, I hardly went to places where gaming was; furthermore, I had no burning desire to gamble even if I was there. Now I occasionally play a game of keno with friends if at a club socially, or very infrequently share a poker machine with some friends for a bit of entertainment. I have no inclination to go to hotels or clubs to either drink or gamble, only as companionship with family and friends for dinner or a social occasion. In fact, I have no desire now to use alcohol or cigarettes, gamble, or partake in any other vice in an attempt to make me feel better. I feel naturally great just the way I am. It is extremely satisfying and empowering knowing you are not reliant on anything or anyone to feel as good as you want to be.

Any one of the many benefits of my success in becoming alcohol-free mentioned above would be reason enough to warrant breaking the habit. Collectively they have certainly been life-changing. However, the greatest benefit is how I now feel about myself. Especially over my last ten years of drinking, my self-image, as well as my perception of what my family, friends, and acquaintances thought of me, had taken a hefty battering. Intrinsically I always wanted to create a good impression on others and to set good moral standards by leading by example. However my behavior while intoxicated often contradicted those standards and counteracted that intent. I used to get so very disappointed with myself after some undesirable experiences that I would feel emotionally and physically sickened. I was living a life of extreme internal conflict. I don't believe I can adequately put into words the deep, core sense of accomplishment, relief, and freedom I feel from overcoming my dependency. The sense of self-respect and satisfaction in my achievement and knowing now I have the power within me to attain anything I make a decision to commit to has been my crowning reward.

I am aware that my assertion and experience that it is possible to fully recover from an alcohol dependency to the point of never desiring a drink again directly contradicts the general cultural wisdom that upholds the mindset of "once an alcoholic, always an alcoholic." This mindset believes that those with a deep alcohol dependency will always be alcoholics in a continual state of recovery and will never be free from relapsing into dependency again. To me, this sounds like the real problem hasn't been dealt with. I certainly know what that feels like: I spent many years expending energy every day worrying about when the next embarrassing episode would occur and trying to keep my drinking habit in control. This was the reason behind my resistance to this approach: if I decided I wanted to stop drinking, I didn't want to then spend the rest of my life worrying about whether I would continue to not drink.

I believe the Alcohemy process that follows finally solves the real problem through a comprehensive process. Although some alcohol dependency support programs provide advice, guidance, and ongoing support to habitual drinkers, I believe my Alcohemy process has a holistic perspective that puts the belief and power back in the hands of the individual not only to stop the behavior of drinking, but also to not desire to use alcohol ever again and to not live in fear of it. Using the Alcohemy process, I now don't feel like I have to be on guard against a relapse at all. I feel totally free from the need or desire to use alcohol for any reason. It would certainly be discouraging to me going into a quit alcohol program believing I would always be considered an alcoholic in an endless state of recovery, constantly being anxious about a relapse waiting around the next corner. What sort of life is that? It seems like just a different, physically healthier version of being mentally stressed. I didn't consider myself to be sick or have some physical or mental illness that I needed medical treatment for. Simply put, I had formed a bad habit of poisoning myself each day, and a side effect of that poison was that it gave me the perception that I felt good and that my circumstances were suddenly okay when I was intoxicated. Over time I became dependent on that delusion, which in turn perpetuated my habit.

I'm not a "recovering alcoholic" now that I have stopped drinking; I live an alcohol-free lifestyle that is now both natural and normal to me. In fact, the only time I was "recovering" was every day that I *was* drinking. Every night that I went to bed and the next day, my body would be recovering from the ethanol poisoning I had caused. My body would immediately go to work desperately trying to eliminate the alcohol and toxins, attempting to undo the damage I had done and regain its health. Then the next afternoon and evening I would top my body up with poison again. When you take all the fancy wrappings, glitter, glamour, and social acceptance away from it, that is exactly what is happening to every person who drinks alcohol.

In my opinion, regular heavy and even frequent social drinkers are actually the real "recovering" alcoholics. I believe my continual state of recovery stopped just a few days after I took my last drink. That is when my body was clear of the alcohol and acetaldehyde (a toxic by-product of alcohol consumption that can lead to severe damage to kidneys and the liver and birth defects). The rest of my process after the first few days was to mentally stay focused on my Alcohemy's alcohol-free plan and strategies, to recondition my brain, and replace my old habits with new healthy ones. I wasn't being poisoned anymore and the toxins were gone. I was now in an adjustment phase and just had to remain committed to the process I had developed.

Now I no longer have any desire to use alcohol for any reason. I have a completely different way of thinking about it now than when I was an alcohol dependent. I understand that the traditional instructions for recovering alcoholics is that alcohol should never pass your lips ever again.

I also understand that if you are relying only on outward abstinence to control alcohol-related problems, then this is very good advice.

What I am about to say next may have purists up in arms. I have had sips of alcohol a few rare times since breaking my dependency. But here's the clincher: I had and continue to have no desire to have another alcoholic drink whatsoever afterward. During these isolated occasions, I chose to have the alcohol for very different reasons than before. It was not as an aid to feel better, to cope with any stress, or to help celebrate an event. It was not because I needed to have it, nor was I depending on the actual alcohol in it to help me with anything. Most were while I was holidaying in South America several years ago, and I tasted a few different local traditional alcoholic drinks on rare occasions, purely to experience the *custom* and very unique *taste*.

However, I strongly advise against doing this unless you have reached the level of certainty that I did and you absolutely know without a doubt that you have no desire to use alcohol again for remedial reasons (psychological or physical). It must only be for purely a single-occasion taste or ritual purpose and never more than a sip. You can't let any self-deception kid you that it is for one of those reasons if deep down you know it isn't.

As for me, I am now in complete and permanent control of my alcohol-related decisions and never consider drinking alcohol socially or as a mood enhancer; "*I am the master of my fate: I am the captain of my soul.*" And that, my friends, is a great success!

The Choice Is Yours

In the midst of my alcohol habit, I spent many years tiptoeing around the problem, content with haphazard attempts at abstinence. But there finally came a moment when the personal cost of drinking exceeded the cost of not drinking. It required a "never-say-die" commitment. Plainly and simply put, it required me to make a choice: Do I want my inner spirit to be in constant bondage, or freedom?

Now it's your turn. You need to ask yourself one question and make one choice. The question is: Do I have at least one good reason why I should stop drinking alcohol? The question is simple and doesn't require any reflection on how small or great a problem you believe your alcohol consumption is. Elements 5 and 6 of my process will expand your thinking on those, though I'm sure most people could come up with one good reason without too much effort right now. Having a strong personal reason (the *why*) is vital to being successful.

Given you have a good reason for stopping, you then have to make one choice: Will I commit uncompromising effort to achieve an alcohol-free lifestyle? If you are only half-hearted or not fair dinkum in your approach, then successful permanent results are unlikely. Alternatively, if you choose to uphold your reasons for becoming alcohol-free and you make the steadfast commitment to actually do it, then meticulously following the thirteen-element plan will do the rest. You can't kid yourself by pretending to be committed if you really are not. You will not have the motivation and drive deep inside to do what it takes. Success takes not only the *why*, the *how*, and *belief*, but also the *commitment* to the required actions. You will get out of life what you put into it. As it was for me, being alcohol-free will be a lifestyle change with immeasurable benefits, and therefore it is worthy of resolute commitment.

If you have answered positively to both your one question and one choice, then start with Element 1 and work your way through each of the following elements in order. Don't take the express train through, taking a glimpse out the window at each stop. Get off at each station and spend some quality time there getting to know yourself better. By deeply reflecting on many of the questions I asked of myself, I felt parts of my soul I hadn't touched in a very long time. Each element serves a vital purpose and helps change you from the inside out. They help with your understanding, reasons, and belief and cement your confidence in place. Spending quality time getting well prepared for your new journey will make the ride much smoother.

Notice I wrote "quality time." This is not 'stalling time' spent procrastinating and stretching out the preparation to avoid actually starting day 1. There is a difference between being well prepared and having everything just perfect. If you wait for everything to be perfect, you will never start. Once you start Element 1, keep the motivation and momentum going as promptly as possible, without rushing. I have no doubt the quality effort you put in going through the thirteen elements will result in improvements to your life and those of loved ones beyond your expectations. That has certainly been my experience, and the doubts, fears, disbeliefs, and anxiety I had about whether I could ever do it and what my life would be like afterward are now mere memories that I revisit only to help others.

Deeply knowing that you have been in control of your process and results the entire way through is the key to the permanency of the Alcohemy solution. It is not a boxed-up, spoon-fed, Band-Aid approach of a temporary nature. I may have developed a framework of thirteen elements to ensure that you understand and complete all the key elements, but it is you who actually has to commit to the serious effort by way of mental preparation, planning, and focused effort. The substance of the Alcohemy solution is not just the sum of each element; it is the synergistic value of all the information in this book that combines to complete the permanent transformation. It's not a product knocked up and pumped out to make a quick buck. Those who are looking for quick, "just add water" effortless fix should put this book down now, and I will gladly refund your purchase price. The solution I offer is for those people that choose to be winners in this new world and are prepared to stand up and take responsibility for their actions and outcomes from here forward. If you desire to hit a home run in life, you better be prepared to learn how to swing the bat yourself and then step up to the plate. Winners are prepared to understand the challenge, focus on the outcome, and commit themselves to doing what it takes. When you boil it down, success or failure are direct results of the many choices we make every single day. *You* can choose to be successful.

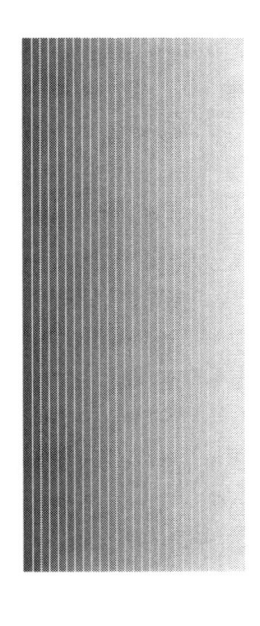

CHAPTER 4

THE REMEDY REVEALED

In this chapter I want to present an overview of the framework of my successful Alcohemy solution and how each element reflects the main key ingredients of why, how, and belief.

As mentioned in the previous chapter, the core framework behind the Alcohemy solution is the comprehensive focus on the why, the how, and belief behind your alcohol habit. I believe that the belief aspect is missing from other programs that assume an alcohol dependency is an irreversible condition you can only at best manage on the surface. Working on principles and techniques to develop your personal belief is part of the end-to-end plan. Also, the why, how, and belief components support and depend on one another—for example, having a solid how plan boosts your belief. Therefore I have written this book not only as a how plan for you, but to present some whys and bolster your belief that you can do it.

As part of my pre-quitting effort I needed to establish the best frame of mind possible, because having the greatest positive outlook and belief was paramount to my success. You also will have to acquire these attitudes if you are choosing to overcome your own habit. I had tried fiddling around trying to manage my habit by adjusting what I drank, when I drank, and how much I drank, though it didn't get me any lasting results. It didn't take away the stress of knowing that sooner or later I would slip up and be very disappointed and embarrassed by yet another alcohol-related incident. What, when, and how much I drank were simply the results of the deeper issue of why I wanted to drink at all in the first place. I had to change my thoughts and feelings about drinking alcohol and what it meant to me. Without changing how I thought and felt about it, I would never change my desire for it. Without changing my desire for it, I would never have the commitment necessary to permanently break my alcohol habit and be alcohol-free.

To address the why, how, and belief behind your alcohol habit, the Alcohemy solution has thirteen elements:

Element 1: Your Journey's History
Element 2: Record Your Associations with Alcohol
Element 3: Record Your Life Values
Element 4: Record What Alcohol Does for You
Element 5: Record the Effects of Ceasing Your Habit
Element 6: Record the Effects of *Not* Ceasing Your Habit
Element 7: Record the Compilation of the Total Effects of Consuming Alcohol versus Current Values
Element 8: Record and Replace Your Fears
Element 9: Record Your Current Actions Involving Alcohol and Replace with New Actions
Element 10: Prepare Answers to Likely Questions and Statements Regarding Your New Habit
Element 11: Write Your Commitment Statement
Element 12: Document and Reward Milestones
Element 13: Plan Your Start Date and *Start*

The human mind is incredibly powerful and can achieve virtually anything it definitely wants to. Given a powerful enough why and belief, it doesn't even really need a known how. It will find a way to make it happen. Fortunately, though, for people reading this book my Alcohemy process gives you a thirteen-element process of how and helps you with your belief throughout the process. Also the first seven elements of the plan help you review and list plenty of reasons why you should cease alcohol consumption. It is entirely up to you which ones have the most meaning for your personal circumstances. After all, this transformation is about you, your habit, and your life, past and future. You need to find the throttle that revs your powerful engine and grab hold of it with both hands. The problem is that most people operate on habitual behavior without really contemplating the whys and why-nots of their routine behavior. Change of any description is considered only when forced by circumstance, rarely by continual self-assessment and desire for constant personal improvement. When circumstances urge change it's usually against our will, outside our comfort zone, and met with resistance, and the search for excuses begins.

To illustrate this, if I was to ask you (as I have others), Do you think you could go three months without having a drink of alcohol? I may well get a lot answers like, "I couldn't go a week without having a drink, let alone three months." However, if I was to legitimately say to most alcohol dependent drinkers, "I have the power and legal authority vested in me to (a) kill the person you love the most, (b) have one of your limbs or other treasured body parts surgically removed, or (c) permanently confiscate all of your finances and worldly possessions if you knowingly have any sip of an alcoholic beverage in the next ninety days." Or, for a positive incentive: "(d) give you US$10 million dollars if you don't knowingly have any sip of an alcoholic beverage in the next ninety days." How many do you think would be able abstain if any of (a) to (d) were possible? Would you be able to abstain under those terms? Even in my heavily dependent drinking days I would have been able to abstain if those conditions were legitimate. You may even know people who have tried unsuccessfully many times to quit smoking, alcohol, drugs, or other addictions, only to quit immediately on receiving advice from their doctor that they only have a short time to live unless they cease. They finally had a why that was more personally important to them then their why to continue.

I understand that the examples mentioned are extreme and grossly confronting, though I'm adamant that we can all do what we ordinarily believe is impossible if we give ourselves a personally important enough reason to accomplish it. It is easy to say you are committed to achieving a goal and then change your mind if the stakes aren't big enough and you have nothing at risk of consequence. In fact, if for some reason (even after reading this book and going through the thirteen-element plan), you are still having difficulty finding a big enough why, mentally make one up, or publicly stake your reputation on the successful outcome. No matter what they are for you, or how you find them, why you are committed to ceasing alcohol must be personally important enough to push you past doubts, fears, and other obstacles.

To understand the first part of the why (i.e., why I felt the desire to start drinking in the first place and why I still believed I needed to) and the real psychological nature of the problem I was dealing with, I needed to gather some information from when I started to drink, right through to where I was now. To do this required me to go back and scrutinize my life from the beginning to see where my associations with alcohol began, how they developed, and why I thought it necessary to use it. This would become Elements 1 and 2.

Now, some people reading this may think this is a bit too over the top or psychoanalytical mumbo-jumbo. However, I assure you these were very important elements in my getting permanent results in overcoming my alcohol dependency. Furthermore, the process was not that difficult to do once I got started, although recalling some of my early childhood memories was not pleasant. You just have to dedicate some quality quiet time to think back and take some short notes on what you remember. One of the difficulties with this part will be actually remembering details around events and incidents that occurred in early childhood and teenage days. For some reading this book, that may be quite some time ago. Also for a few (including me), some of these memories may be particularly unpleasant and may have been purposely buried and blocked from conscious thought as much as possible. I believe if you do as I did and approach this as an analytical exercise, plus view those unpleasant events as a movie in your mind as if you were an outside observer and not an active participant, you will see and review them more objectively. Try to view them as historic events that you are professionally analyzing rather than immersing yourself into the emotional feelings again. Regardless of whether you have distressing memories or not, if you dedicate sufficient quiet time to relax and think back in time while asking yourself "What are my early memories of *[area of focus]*?" then these will eventually come to you.

If your history contains memories of things you did that you are embarrassed or ashamed of, you have to realize that you are not the same person now and let those feelings go. We *all* make mistakes and have done things we wish we hadn't. I have done quite a few unacceptable and very regrettable things in my life, and not all of them have been recounted in this book. All of these poor choices and actions were taken out of frustration, desperation, ignorance, or alcohol-impaired judgment.

Feeling guilt for the rest of your life serves no purpose at all and is one of the most self-destroying feelings there is. You need to understand that every one of us is always trying to do the best we can relevant to our preconditioned belief systems and level of knowledge and enlightenment; and that includes you. We *always* act in ways that we perceive will make us feel better. If you did something that you subsequently felt guilty about, that means you have learned from the experience that it is not something you would like to do again, therefore you are now a subtly different person.

Every experience we have changes us in some way. Embrace your new self for recognizing the mistake and learning the lesson, then forgive your old self and let the guilt go. It may seem improper to some, though even if you are feeling guilty about something you knew was wrong before you actually did it, you still need to forgive yourself because you obviously didn't have the psychological comprehension and life skills to act in any other way. Spending the rest of your life trying to make up for the past will not change it. It only serves to keep you bound to it and prevents you from moving on. The important thing is that you recognize it was wrong, learn from it, and commit to behave more appropriately in the future.

You should use this same reasoning to forgive others who have done things you are unhappy about, as they also were only acting at their level of personal development and psychological understanding. They too are always acting in ways that they perceive will make themselves feel better. It doesn't make what they had done 'right' or 'acceptable' in any way, though you do have to let go of it being a negative influence on your present life. Let the wrongdoing and the consequences remain where they belong (with the perpetrator) and not with you. Your values and power should remain unharmed and in complete control of your thoughts and actions.

It is a worldwide tragedy we all don't realize that the very best way to make ourselves feel better, is to make others feel better. It has been shown in scientific experiments that when a person does an act of kindness toward someone else, the person who commits the act of kindness has a rise in dopamine and serotonin levels (which makes them feel good). Furthermore, so does the person who receives the act of kindness and, even more interesting, so does anyone witnessing the kind act. The lesson here is that to make yourself feel better naturally, simply do kind things to other people and surround yourself with kind-minded people.

The second part of the why component is why you want to stop drinking alcohol. This is the most critical part of the why. If you don't have one or more reasons that are extremely important to you personally, your commitment and ability to overcome challenges may not be strong enough to get you through the early days. You need at least one, and preferably more, of these whys that mean so much to you personally that failure is not an option. If you want to stop drinking only because someone else wants you to, then you won't have the internal strength to see you through challenging temptations. Furthermore, because it is someone else's reason (not yours), there is a high possibility your resentment will build against them as you struggle and fight against your real desire to keep drinking. Your own spirit and desire must be the driving force behind your thoughts and actions. When challenged and confronted by obstacles and temptations, your personal whys are what will keep your unwavering resolve in place. When the going gets tough, failures often look for excuses to quit and attribute the reason to someone or something else. It will be easy for you to think, *Oh well, I didn't really want to do it anyway; it wasn't really my idea.* Winners and successful people on the other hand have their own very strong, personal reasons why they want to achieve their goals and commit to them on those grounds, regardless of what others may think or say.

The next historic information that I used included the personal values I had developed over the years (Element 3). I believe we get most of our values from our parents or people we trust when we are very young. I wanted to review what they were and whether they were valid and helpful to me now. It had occurred to me that most of the behaviors resulting from excessive alcohol consumption would not align with my core values; hence it would be very helpful to write them down and review why. To lead a truly harmonious life we should have decent, life-enhancing values, and our beliefs and actions should all align with them. If they are not aligned (and mine weren't), then we need to spend quality time to review and resolve why they are not. So I listed what values I had when I was young and compared them to what I had now.

Having spent time systematically reviewing my alcohol associations and significant events from my younger years through to the present, along with reviewing what values I had adopted during that time, I was able to re-examine some beliefs I'd learned and see if they were aligned to my present values. Again, this may seem tedious or too much effort to some, though I assure you the more you understand how you were thinking then and are thinking now, the better prepared you will be to make the permanent changes required for your success. I have included templates in the appendix for you to copy and fill in the blanks. Alternatively you can download an electronic version at www.alcohemy.com.

There will be some people that state that they are not deep thinkers and have trouble answering the why questions like "Why did I do that?" or "Why do I believe this?" Furthermore there will be some who simply answer why questions with evasive and cop-out answers like "I don't know" or "Because that's just the way I do it" or "It seemed like the right thing at the time." It's either because they are too mentally lazy to make the effort to really think, or they have not realized there is an answer that will help with future decisions.

I suggest you give it your very best shot and spend some quality time trying to authentically think beyond the events to the reasons why. You are going to live your life either by self-design or by default to whatever whim comes your way. The people who aren't interested in genuinely thinking about why they have been and are presently doing things mostly run on automatic, and they will unlikely ever be the masters of their fate. It's really not that hard when you set aside some quiet time and get started. Most are just not used to it. Ask yourself some 'why' and some 'what if' questions to start with, or ask those type of questions when you are thinking back on a particular situation. If you give yourself some time and focus, you will be surprised at how much you really do know and can answer. Quite often the answers that surface will lead to more why questions, and the answers to those lead to the core of the situation. The secret is to not quit querying. The more you understand why you have done or are doing certain things, the more you are likely to be in control and therefore be the captain of your soul.

Next I asked myself a series of questions designed to reveal the perceived advantages versus disadvantages of drinking (Elements 4, 5, 6, and 7) and also what fears I had relating to my alcohol dependency (Element 8). By seriously pondering these questions and being brutally honest with my answers, I was able to clearly see by my resulting notes how unnecessary, irrational, and counterproductive consuming alcohol was.

Some of these conclusions may have already been realized from the mental questioning and answering during the previous exercises. Nonetheless each of these slightly different reviews was very necessary for it to be irrefutably shown in written form how needless and irrelevant alcohol was for me to live a happy life. Moreover, it was having a detrimental effect on my life by causing considerable grief and stress, along with holding me back in areas of personal development and creativity I was keen to pursue.

I believed that not only would it be important to have mentally considered these questions and answers, but also it would be imperative that I record them to regularly review when carrying out my commitment to stop drinking. I wanted to have irrefutable reasons in my face just in case my resolve to stop drinking wavered during the early stages of ceasing.

My plan was to use these positive motives as mental fortification against cravings and possible withdrawal symptoms I was anticipating.

Thankfully, my cravings and symptoms of withdrawal weren't near as bad as I had previously conjured up in my mind that they would be. I am convinced this was due to the psychological self-analysis process I had completed prior to ceasing. Furthermore I believe this work had created such a strong desire and commitment in me to cease alcohol that my brain produced overriding biochemical responses to make the abstinence less distressing. (This was my personal experience, and I recommend that anyone who experiences tremors or a severe reaction to alcohol withdrawal seek medical advice.)

Another Alcohemy element that was also crucial to my success was to have some alternate measures in place to deal with situations and events that would usually trigger the desire for an alcoholic drink (Element 9). These are the times that I would most likely be tempted or feeling the urge or craving to have a drink. Also, it is crucial to plan ahead in anticipation of certain friends and family members actively opposing or being a negative influence regarding your new intention to live an alcohol-free life (Element 10). Anticipating these temptations and influences and planning answers and statements to others' inevitable questions about your new lifestyle is critical to your long-term success, and I will cover this in detail later.

To cement my newly planned actions and behaviors in place, I literally contracted myself to follow through with a written and signed commitment statement (Element 11). I treated this as a formal and binding contract with my integrity that I would do whatever was necessary to be successful regardless of what challenges I encountered. Make a formal commitment that is personal and meaningful for your own personal circumstances.

I also planned specific rewards for achievement milestones planned in advance of my start date (Element 12). These are very important as they give you some short-term goals to focus on while your confidence may be weak and uncertain. As you reach these early milestones, your confidence and belief grow stronger, and therefore later milestones can be spread further apart. The great effort and focus required at the start should be rewarded by celebrating your success at very short intervals. This signals to your brain and body that you have been successful, and dopamine and serotonin are released, making you feel good about that accomplishment. The more often you celebrate and reward yourself for your success, the more often dopamine will be released. This not only replaces some of the regular dopamine that was released due to the alcohol you used to drink; it also reinforces to your brain that you are now doing a good thing and that it would be advantageous to make a habit of it.

If all our desires in life could be achieved with ease and little effort, there would be no satisfaction experienced in their attainment. There would be very little dopamine or serotonin release. Doing most things would become a matter of course, unfulfilling and boring. Fortunately, we experience psychological and physical rewards proportionate to the amount of effort it has taken us to successfully achieve something. Accomplishing things of little consequence gives us little reward. Conversely, achieving something that has taken considerable personal effort delivers an equally large amount of personal satisfaction and reward. At the beginning of this journey even small steps of one day may take considerable personal effort and determination, depending on your individual circumstances. If this is the case for you, be generous to yourself and not only accept the psychological sense of satisfaction that comes with these small steps, but also treat yourself to a healthy form of physical reward. The greater the amount of energy and determination required, reward yourself with a proportionate level of acknowledgment of your success.

The principle is no different from the amount of fuss and admiration Donna and I bestowed upon our two boys after they first used the toilet by themselves. It was a big step for them in toilet training, and they were generously praised for succeeding and to encourage the continued behavior. However, now that they are young adults, I can assure you we don't wait outside and bestow the same acclamations upon them now after they visit the loo. It all has to do with the amount of personal effort and achievement of the individual involved. The bigger and more arduous the task at hand is for you personally, the closer together you should make your milestones and rewards. This keeps your level of satisfaction with your progress higher and elevates your motivation to persist.

I used this method of breaking big tasks requiring considerable and sustained mental and physical effort into small sections when I was doing triathlons and marathon running. Instead of looking at the whole race and the huge effort involved in its entirety, I would focus on and acknowledge the completion of small sections of it at a time. For example, if I was running along a flat road I would focus on a point maybe fifty meters (fifty-five yards) in front of me; then, when I had successfully completed that, I would focus on the next fifty meters. If I came to a very steep hill, I might reduce my focus down to as little as two meters (just over two yards) in front of me and recognize my success with each of these sections with a mental *Yes! Next!* I would do this two-meter focus section after section until I was at the top of the hill. It signaled frequent positive feedback to my brain, which in turn produced the necessary biochemical and physical reactions to reward me again and again, hence the steep hill didn't seem so grueling. If I was at the top of a long downhill gradient where the effort required would be comparably very easy, I would look as far ahead as I could see and think to myself "I have all this downhill distance to cruise along to recover a bit mentally and physically," again using it like a positive reward. That way I was always focusing on what I believed were achievable chunks, and my mind was regularly thinking success and reward after each of them, which in turn created the expectation of more success and reward.

This is the process I used in my Alcohemy plan, and I suggest you do also. At the start it will appear like a very steep and daunting hill that will require more focus and effort, therefore your immediate goals and reward milestones should be very short. I suggest (as I did) you make each day for at least a week a separate milestone. Mark it off on a timeline chart at the end of each day and at the very least give yourself a mental pat on the back as a reward. Perhaps even a scrumptious food or beverage each day as a reward and dopamine release. After the first week I went to one-week milestones until my next key thirty-day target was reached. This was my brain reset, the milestone I set to know when I had indeed changed my old alcohol consumption habit to a new habit of not using alcohol. From that point I knew I had changed my habitual behavior and now just needed to be vigilant for circumstances and factors that were previously strong triggers to drink alcohol. After my first thirty days my milestones were two months, three months, six months, one year, and two years, and it has been no more than an annual reflection after that, given it is well and truly normal life for me now.

Finally, once you have all these elements completed in detail and planned accordingly, all that remains is to plan a start date and start following your plan (Element 13).

You Must Begin with Belief

In summary, the most important element is to have the *belief* that you can be totally alcohol-free. The belief that something can be achieved is the main and most powerful element in actually achieving it. For over half my life deep down I knew I had an alcohol dependency problem, though I did nothing about it apart from some temporary consumption management strategies. The issue was that I didn't really believe that could or would ever stop drinking altogether.

It is one thing knowing it is a problem (which is important), and that you should do something about it. However, it is another matter believing that you have what it takes to live alcohol-free and to actually make a resolute commitment then see it through to the end. I did not see myself as a non-drinker and could not envisage never having another glass of red wine, bourbon, or beer. The logic of not drinking was sound (given that the human mind and body were designed to function better without alcohol), though I perceived that to be so unattainable for me personally that it wasn't even an option. It wasn't until I started to believe it was possible that I started to consider how I might achieve it and what it would mean for my life.

Once I realized that a lot of life is made up of a series of habits and that habits can be created, changed, or stopped, I had started on the right track. I also reasoned that my alcohol dependency started from drinking as a regular pastime and was now just a bad habit on steroids. Therefore, as with all habits, I had the power to change or stop it altogether. With this in mind, along with continued reading about human behavior, my belief that I could become alcohol independent was established.

My interest continued to grow and I have now read many books and research documents and listened to audio programs detailing how belief affects not only our psychology, but also our physiology. This has been demonstrated time and time again in scientific research and trials where placebos are used. In many cases where the test subjects believed they would respond in a certain emotional and/or physical way, their brain responded by creating that actual result.

As an example, some experiments were done at an American university where trial subjects were told they were given alcoholic drinks, when in fact the drinks had no alcohol in them. After a few drinks, the subjects reported experiencing the usual array of effects from alcohol consumption. Another group were told they were having drinks that contained no alcohol, when in fact there was a standard measure of alcohol in each drink. After several drinks, most of these subjects reported no effect of alcohol whatsoever. In each case, it was the belief that had caused the brain and body to react accordingly.

I believe that combining my pre-ceasing process with my new belief that my dependency was a habit that could be broken, plus my determination and expectation of success, resulted in my brain biochemically assisting me in my quest. I was looking for and focused on positive results, and my brain and body responded with mental and physical evidence to support my success.

There is an excellent book called *The Biology of Belief* by Bruce H. Lipton, a published and internationally recognized authority in bridging science and spirit and a leading voice in new biology, which goes in to great detail on how our environment, including our thoughts, directly affect the behavior of our body's cells. He explains from a scientific perspective how our perceptions of the world around us and of our circumstances govern not only our behaviors, but also our body's cellular and chemical makeup. This in turn helps determine our health and the quality of our life. His findings tie in beautifully with what I found and experienced once my perception of my alcohol habit changed (by working through my Alcohemy process of why, how, and belief).

His scientific explanation also goes hand in glove with my belief that by understanding I had old subconscious programs controlling my behaviors, then changing myself from the inside first, before attempting to cease alcohol, my own body started producing the physical actions at a cellular and chemical level to help achieve the results I so deeply desired. I urge anyone wanting to examine human potential and bolster the belief that they can control the quality of his or her life to get a copy. I wish I had it available years ago to help me with mine.

To further substantiate the power of belief I have read some amazing accounts reported by well-respected medical and psychology professionals in which people's beliefs have produced physical results beyond normal explanation. There have been many reports of people conquering and healed of "incurable" illnesses when medical science could not, people making miraculous recoveries from spinal and other serious physical injuries when medical professionals said was impossible. The one thing common to these people was the determined and focused belief that they would get better. In some cultures belief was used to actually kill people. Some versions of voodoo, witchcraft, or spells used strong belief to cause physical harm or death. In Australia the traditional Aboriginal *kurdaitcha* man would use a 'point the bone' ritual as revenge or punishment for a serious offence and the victim would usually become gravely ill and die. There was nothing physically done to the person; it was the vehement belief in the spiritual ritual that caused their physical demise.

Some of my favorite examples of how a person's absolute belief can change his or her psychological and physical reality are ones involving people with Multiple Personality Disorder, now called Dissociated Identity Disorder (DID). Bruce Lipton also uses the Dissociated Identity Disorder condition to emphasize how absolute belief can affect and change our physiology and chemistry. While in the different personalities, DID sufferers have separate psychological and belief identities. Each personality shares the same physical body, though has its own reality. It has been reported that while, for example, personality A is active, the person may safely enjoy eating certain foods and can use certain prescription drugs, while in personality B the same body may actually have a severe allergic reaction if they eat the same food or take the same drug. It was documented where one DID person presented to a doctor with an extreme allergic reaction to a wasp sting. A short time later when in a different personality the swelling and reaction disappeared, only to return again when the personality changed back again. Physical attributes like taste, hearing, sight, chronic illness, injuries, pain, hormone levels, and voice can change within minutes or seconds when the belief of who the personality changes. These are real physical aspects that can't be faked or explained away as a psychological act. Some DID suffers even change the color of their eyes between personalities.

These examples may seem extreme, though I consider them to be excellent instances of how powerful having absolute belief can be. Most of us don't access that level of belief in our day-to-day lives, though when presented with a significant challenge it is very important to our success, that we develop and maintain a strong belief in a successful outcome. Your values and beliefs govern your thoughts, your dominant thoughts elicit your feelings and emotions, your feelings and emotions regulate your commitment and drive your actions, and your actions determine your results. This sequence can form a loop with the results you achieve either strengthening or sometimes challenging existing beliefs, depending on the result. Though you can target any individual area of this sequence to make significant changes to your results, nothing is more powerful than your belief.

One of the main purposes of writing this book is to help give other people with an alcohol dependency the belief they can be alcohol-free, and letting them know that being liberated from it is so very much better than they may imagine. The lack of belief that I could ever do it was my primary barrier to even considering giving it a go. Once I had the belief I could do it, my mind went to work on fathoming the nuts and bolts of how to do it. Not only did my belief help manifest ideas on how to best accomplish my desire to be rid of my alcohol habit; it produced the biochemical support to aid my success. The belief that I could achieve it and the belief that my day-to-day life would become much better than it was were the catalysts in getting me to blissful alcohol-free state I am in today. The process summarized above and covered in more detail in the next chapter is what cemented in my mind that my alcohol-free future would be better than my current existence. It changed my original perception that a life without regular drinking would be unsociable, boring, and a constant struggle to abstain to a belief that the real me would always be present and I would be free from every alcohol-related stress and insecurity I was currently feeling. I would be free to confidently progress my life in all the positive directions I wished to take.

Although I had absorbed quite a bit of knowledge on how the human mind and behavior functioned from personal development books and recordings, simply knowing these general principles was not enough to successfully cease my alcohol habit. I needed a step-by-step process that applied directly to the specific behavior of alcohol consumption, tailored to my particular history and circumstances. This is exactly what my Alcohemy process did for me, and what it can do for you.

Tips Before You Get Started
When you decide to begin the Alcohemy process, I suggest you dedicate some time periods of at least thirty minutes when and where you can be free completely from distractions. You should schedule this time, for if you wait for a convenient time to come around, it never will. This time will be one of the most important investments in your future life and success you can make, so give it that sort of priority. Preferably be in a place where you can relax comfortably and let your mind wander from the present environment. You will need to be relaxed enough to revisit your earliest memories and the thoughts and feelings you had at those times. Driving in traffic situations while doing this may not be wise for safety reasons. Also it would be advantageous if you are in a place where you able to jot down short notes about your memories, thoughts, and feelings as they come to mind.

To answer the questions honestly in some of the exercises of this process you really must stop and take quality time to connect with your true self, not the perception of yourself that is obtained from some fleeting, shallow thoughts of who you would like to be. You must connect and answer the following exercises openly and honestly from the deeper core of who you truly feel you are right now. Some of the questions and answers in my process were personally very confronting. It would have been easy to water down my answers to feel better about myself and pamper my ego, though that would be self-defeating in my effort to make real and permanent change. I strongly encourage you ask the tough and confronting questions of yourself and to be brutally honest with your answers. Only by doing this will you be able to face and commit to systematically changing your thoughts, actions, and results to positive ones. If you choose to make excuses, feel sorry for yourself, or start playing the victim role (no matter what your previous circumstances were), you will not have the right attitude to be in control of this process and will continue to be governed by external circumstances.

What follows are the thirteen detailed elements to complete before you begin your lifelong commitment to the cessation of drinking alcohol. I suggest you read through the entire book first, then come back and complete these elements in their numbered order. To do so, you can download a free copy of the Element Workbook, which includes space to work through each of the thirteen elements, at www.alcohemy.com. Don't take any shortcuts, especially if you find the first eight elements confronting, as these are the elements that will help you achieve *permanent* results by changing yourself from within. If you embrace those, the rest of the process will be much easier.

PART TWO

THE ALCOHEMY PROCESS

ELEMENT 1

YOUR JOURNEY'S HISTORY

Once I reached the stage where I knew I *needed* to stop being dependent on alcohol, likewise I *desired* to live in a new and better way without alcohol, and I had also made the *decision* to do whatever it took to find out how, I determined the best starting point was to take a journey back to my earliest memories to see how it may have all started. I already had the basic understanding that I drank alcohol to feel good (or at least improve how I currently felt), and over the years this practice became a deep-rooted habit. It was like a huge noxious weed in my life's garden that was slowly but surely overpowering and choking out any flowers of happiness and success. Its vine-like foliage had reached into all areas of my life, strangling my desires and the great potential we all have. I figured if I could work out where and why those roots began, I would have my best chance of completely removing the need for this toxic alcohol weed; foliage, stem, roots, and all.

The Alcohol Weed

This weed plant represents your alcohol habit (or any destructive habit, for that matter) and the basic components of it. Like any plant, this alcohol habit weed needs a structure and nourishment to ensure and sustain its survival, growth, and perpetuation. The parts of this weed below the ground are likened to your inner workings, such as your beliefs, desires, and emotions either conscious or subconscious. Everything above the ground is the manifestation or result of what is under the surface and the interactions with your visible physical world.

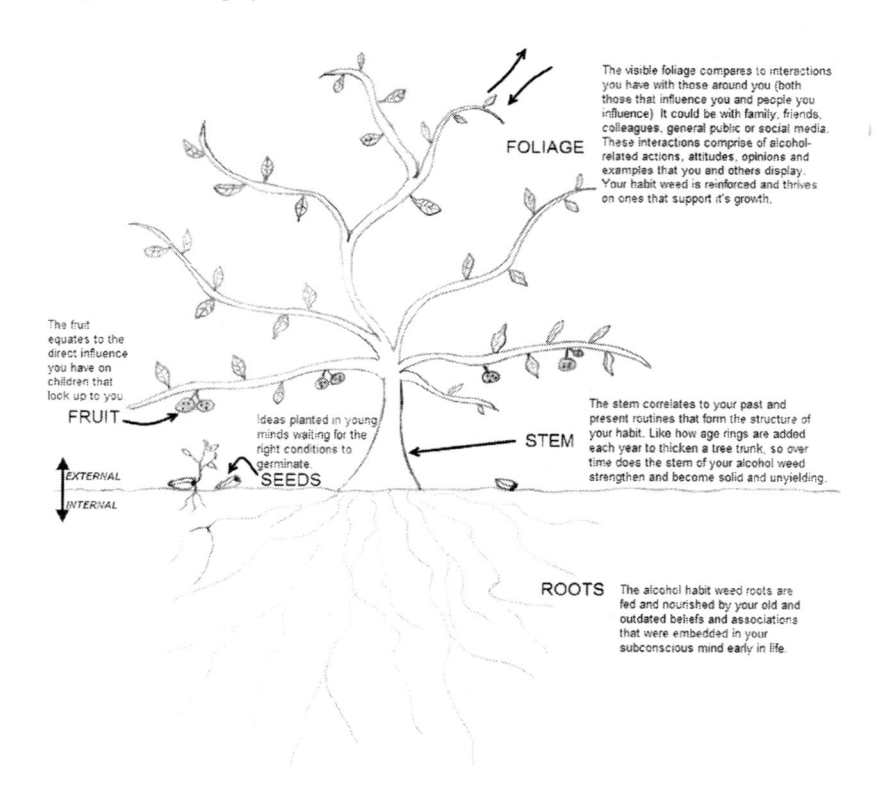

FOLIAGE — The visible foliage compares to interactions you have with those around you (both those that influence you and people you influence). It could be with family, friends, colleagues, general public or social media. These interactions comprise of alcohol-related actions, attitudes, opinions and examples that you and others display. Your habit weed is reinforced and thrives on ones that support it's growth.

FRUIT — The fruit equates to the direct influence you have on children that look up to you.

SEEDS — Ideas planted in young minds waiting for the right conditions to germinate.

STEM — The stem correlates to your past and present routines that form the structure of your habit. Like how age rings are added each year to thicken a tree trunk, so over time does the stem of your alcohol weed strengthen and become solid and unyielding.

ROOTS — The alcohol habit weed roots are fed and nourished by your old and outdated beliefs and associations that were embedded in your subconscious mind early in life.

EXTERNAL / INTERNAL

Seed

Most plants reproduce from either seeds or rhizomes deposited by a parent plant. In this case I will use a seed analogy. The seed in this case represents the seed of thought that was planted in your subconscious mind with your earliest associations with alcohol use. Somewhere, somehow you originally developed the belief that using alcohol was a benefit to you and an acceptable option to enhance feeling good. This may have been planted while you were very young by observing alcohol consumption by your family, in social media and advertising, or a combination of sources. The seed was easily planted in your young, impressionable, and fertile mind and lay dormant, awaiting germination. Some of your earliest whys began at this stage. The germination was a result of two conditions being favorable: You needed to feel the desire to use alcohol for some reason, and you need access to it. The desire may come from your conditioned belief that drinking is an adult activity, and you want to feel more adult. It may be that you are trying to block out some emotional pain. The desire to try it is not enough alone; you need access to alcohol. More than likely this was when you reached an age when you were considered old enough to start consuming alcohol at family social occasions. Maybe it was when you and your friends could obtain and consume alcohol without parents or other adults knowing. Perhaps your alcohol habit seed didn't germinate until you reached the legal drinking age. Either way, the seed of thought that consuming alcohol is a benefit started rapidly spreading roots when you began putting it into practice. I don't believe we will ever stop the seeds of alcohol use from being planted in young minds, and most young people will at some stage try it.

Roots

By starting and continuing to consume alcohol, your fledgling weed seedling's roots grew quickly. As you confirmed in your mind that alcohol did have a legitimate place in your life, your belief system nourished these roots, enabling them to become large and strong. It probably didn't matter too much in these early years whether consuming alcohol was a smart or healthy thing to do, because we all feel ten feet tall and bulletproof at that age. If we see others experiencing some negative side effects, we don't think it will be a long-term problem for us. As we continue to consume and mentally validate alcohol's use—for reasons like stress relief; to feel happy, confident, or popular at social occasions; or to attempt to block out unpleasant memories—then habit roots continue to grow and strengthen.

Our internal beliefs and misconceptions that alcohol use is necessary or a benefit to us emotionally and physically nourish the weed via this internal root system. Our continued desire to use alcohol because of our misguided perception that ethanol makes us feel better, happy, or relaxed is the lifeblood of the alcohol habit weed.

The roots are everything that lies beneath the surface. So in this case the roots are your internal conscious and subconscious thoughts and beliefs, past and present. These are unresolved or perhaps partly resolved things that prompted you to look for alternatives to natural, healthy ways of obtaining happiness and comfort, things that most likely but not necessarily happened during your preteen, adolescent, and early adult years. Without excellent, compatible, and trustworthy role models for young people to learn healthy coping strategies, it is easy for them to learn and adopt other inappropriate ones to help deal with the many issues they face at these times of physical and emotional growth. Young people will watch and learn from those they are closest to or admire. These are most likely family members, relatives, and friends, though they could also be characters they like on television or people they know through social media. If these role models are not demonstrating and encouraging healthy attributes and ways to deal with life's challenges, then it is likely that young and impressionable people will follow their poor examples.

The key to preventing an alcohol or any negative habit from growing, and especially to destroy an existing habitual dependence, is to uproot the weed and deprive the roots of any suitable nourishment. This is the purpose of the Alcohemy process I developed. Deep down I knew I had to change the way I thought about drinking alcohol, including invalidating even my earliest whys. I realized I had to thoroughly examine my beliefs, including when I had formed them and why. I became convinced that unless I made changes at that deeper, inner level, I would never permanently change. I was right! By following my process, I now think about alcohol consumption in a totally different way. I have no desire whatsoever to depend on alcohol or the altered states of mind it gave me. As soon as I cut off the inappropriate emotional desires and beliefs to the weed root system, the rest of the habit plant wilted and died within a month or two. This will be the key to your success also. Without viable roots the habit weed stem and foliage can't survive.

Stem

The parts of the alcohol habit weed that we see above the ground consist of the stem, foliage, and fruit. These are the visual and non-physical results of drinking alcohol in the form of interactions and influences associated with the habit. I liken the stem of the alcohol weed to the routine structure of your habit. The stem is made up of your typical daily, weekly, and situational practices and actions associated with consuming alcohol, the day-in, day-out usual behaviors that you find yourself automatically doing when you have an opportunity to consume alcohol. It is how your habit manifests in the world, including when and how much you drink. As with most plant stems, the alcohol habit weed stem is fairly robust and stable. It is the basic noticeable part of your behavior that connects and is nourished by both the roots (internal beliefs and desires) and foliage (external influences). The longer the habit weed grows, the bigger, stronger, and more stable the core supportive stem structure becomes. Just like the age rings in a tree trunk keep expanding out in number with age, so does the weed stem strengthen with time.

A mistake I made for many years was thinking that if I could somehow manage and restrict my physical drinking behavior (placing a constriction around the alcohol weed habit stem), then my dependency would be in control. Furthermore, I incorrectly assumed that by merely interrupting my drinking for a period of time (cutting right through the stem), I would have even more control and start afresh. Both of these efforts were doomed to fail, for as with most plants if you simply constrict or even cut the stem through, leaving a viable root system in place, the plant will simply grow around the constriction or readily sprout healthy foliage again from the cut stem. This is exactly what happened to me. My internal alcohol root system (my whys) was still feeding my desire to drink, and my weed stem overcame any management strategies I used. It was through this trial and error that I came to the realization that the secret to success lay in removing the roots, not merely restricting the stem (habit routine).

Foliage

I equate the branches and leaves of the alcohol weed plant to the interactions and influences related to your alcohol habit. Just as a plant's foliage absorbs carbon dioxide from and expels oxygen into its surrounding environment, there is a two-way flow of physical and non-physical communication with people and situations in your environment. We constantly give out verbal and nonverbal signals and receive information and feedback in the same manner, whether solicited or not. We form impressions and opinions of others and they do of us based on these signals. Because this particular plant is a noxious alcohol habit weed, its equivalent to carbon dioxide is any feedback it can absorb and metabolize (rationalize) that confirms that drinking alcohol is a benefit and a good habit. It thrives on this input and transports this down to the internal root (belief) system to help nourish and reinforce those beliefs. This in turn provides better growth and an even stronger stem (physical habit) and foliage (interaction and influence). Unfortunately, unlike other harmless and beneficial plants found in a garden, the toxic alcohol weed does not expel anything good. Instead of valuable oxygen, the gas this noxious weed expels is simply more of the same toxic feedback and unfitting validation to others, feedback that you also condone and that supports the use of alcohol to help meet your physical and emotional needs and desires.

This is one of the reasons people with alcohol dependences regularly congregate together. They thrive on each other's feedback (expelled gas) via their social interactions and influence (foliage). This in turn reinforces their belief (root system) that drinking alcohol is a good and appropriate thing to do. They get a comfortable amount of environmental support (nourishment) from gathering in groups of people with the same habit (group of same weed species creating a gaseous atmosphere that supports their foliage). If you were to put a single alcohol-dependent weed in the middle of a garden full of flowers, it wouldn't have the right atmosphere to flourish. Similarly, if you put a single person with a heavy alcohol dependence into party of people who don't drink alcohol, that person would be very uncomfortable and would more than likely want to leave. Correspondingly, if you put a single non-drinker into a room full of people who are eagerly consuming alcohol and displaying signs of intoxication, then that person would not be comfortable, as this environment would not be suitable to them. Where habits are concerned, weeds prefer the company of weeds, and flowers prefer flowers.

The foliage and branches of an alcohol habit weed can take on a vine-like nature, extending into all areas of your life, including family, work, social circles, and community. The two-way interaction and influences mainly have negative consequences. Examples of these may be conversations or actions due to poor behavioral or attitude displays, violence, relationship problems with a partner, family or friends, work performance issues, and inappropriate or antisocial activity within your community. There may not even be any physical conversation or visible action take place, rather a conscious or subconscious influence or opinion ensues as a result of an alcohol-related behavior which has an impact on you or another. Relationship breakdowns, friendships hurt, careers ruined, community respect damaged and loss of self-esteem can all happen either very quickly or gradually depending on the alcohol-related behavior and situation. The weed habit foliage is the main mechanism which you affect and influence others, plus people in turn acknowledge and respond to you either positively or negatively.

Trying to manage or control an alcohol dependency by limiting or controlling the interactions you have with people around you is not going to produce a change to your habit. It is no different in that regard to pruning or trimming the branches of a plant. It will only temporarily reduce the amount of foliage and therefore the interactions with other people. The roots (belief) or stem (core habit actions) don't change, and when the conditions are right, new foliage shoots out and grows back to be as thick and bushy as it was before. Hiding yourself away and limiting your interactions with others only confines the visibility of the habit and associated problems to those close to you. I can vouch for this, as limiting my social exposure was one of the failed management strategies I'd used. When I finally realized that there must be some substance to the honest negative feedback I got from my immediate family and occasional ribbing and jibes from friends about my states of intoxication, my reaction to this embarrassment was to simply reduce my social interactions. I figured that what people didn't know about they couldn't comment on—problem solved, I thought. No, not at all. The alcohol weed habit will survive quite well with just the healthy root system, stem, and a few leaves intact. I still had the habit, only now my family and very close friends knew the real truth. I severely pruned my interaction foliage back even further, to permit myself to drink as much as I really wanted only on occasions when I was completely alone or in a place where I was positive no one personally knew me. I reasoned that no one I cared about would know about my excessive drinking binge except me, and they wouldn't think ill of me if they didn't know. It did nothing to curb my desire to consume inappropriate levels of alcohol. As you can tell by this example, managing the foliage isn't a permanent solution as it won't kill the habit weed.

Fruit

I have included the fruit of the habit weed plant in this analogy because, although it is similar to the foliage in that it influences others, it is one-way communication and is particularly relevant to those very close to you. I liken the fruit (containing seeds) of the weed plant to your behavioral actions that are observable to those people in your immediate area of influence, especially ones that are impressionable and readily accept your leadership. Children are prime examples, as they readily observe, gather, and accept verbal and nonverbal information (fruit) from parents, relatives, and other adults they trust and admire. They are the ones most reliant on and trusting of the protection and shelter of your canopy. The behavioral examples and role modeling these older, trusted, respected, or admired people provide are like seed-bearing fruit falling onto very fertile soil (impressionable minds). This fruit should be nothing but the best for these impressionable minds, but the fruit that hangs down from the alcohol weed is not fit for them. The conditions may not be right for germination into a habit at this time, though the seeds will remain dormant in the fertile soil until the right conditions are met. It is reported that a lot of the behaviors and habits that a young person will develop or have a predilection for will be learned by observation of other admired people's actions at a very early age. We as parents or mentors can explain to a child that consuming alcohol is not good for your health; however, if we ourselves are behaving contrary to that, the child will take more notice of our behavior than our words. The fruit truly does not fall and germinate too far from the tree. If we are going to be great role models for our children and other minds we influence, we had better be willing to lead by example, practice what we preach, and walk the talk. It is too late once the fruit has been ingested or has fallen from the weed plant awaiting germination. Before your habit plant reaches maturity, you had better decide whether the fruit it bears will reproduce weeds or flowers in your garden.

It is never too late to remove the weeds, roots and all, and replace them with flowers. An alcohol habit weed can only be completely and permanently removed if the root system is destroyed. Anything less will not result in an enduring and satisfactory result. Permanent changes to our habitual behavior need to begin with an evaluation of our past and present beliefs and actions. Only by changing our inner beliefs and feelings about our behaviors can we expect to see permanent changes to our external actions.

Therefore, in Element 1, our primary task is to fully examine the root structure of the alcohol habit weed, so it can be removed completely.

Examining Your Emotional Past

To fully understand how I ended up with the negative alcohol habit I developed, I needed to go back to the beginning, way back in time to my earliest memories to reflect and examine why I felt the need to gain some perceived comfort or benefit from external substances such as alcohol. It is a journey you must take to unearth the core reasons for the beliefs you now have, some of which are fossilized under the sediment of perhaps years of emotional conditioning or indoctrinated behavior. Most people develop most of their substance dependencies or habits in an attempt either to gain some pleasurable feeling or excitement that is lacking in their present life, or to feel better by suppressing negative experiences in their past. It may well be a combination of these, depending on the circumstances of your upbringing and current situation. Regardless, I determined it was important for me to re-examine my entire life from early childhood to present, not to dwell on the negative aspects, but more to see what triggered my desire for alcohol and therefore to be able to simply acknowledge and let it go. I needed to be in control of my life and not be governed by things that happened in my past.

Some of these memories I had never discussed with others, as some of the more traumatic memories are of my parents' relationship and other sensitive family circumstances. But I took the time to reflect on these memories and reviewed them in a more objective light. I recalled them as if I were watching an old movie that I wasn't in. That way I could distance myself from the emotional pain and be more objective. Before acquiring a more enlightened understanding, I used to mentally cringe and desperately and immediately try to erase any tormenting memories whenever they came up. But as I was learning and mastering a greater array of skills in liberating my mind, I was able to drill deep into my subconscious and analyze some of the more distressing memories.

Regardless of what your past was like, it is important to take an intimate journey back to reflect on the times when you were particularly happy, sad, or angry. Some of these negative issues will be helpful in determining why you resorted to using alcohol to feel better, while some of the positive events will reveal the nature of your true self, currently choked out by the noxious weed of your alcohol habit. Your specific questions are listed at the end of the chapter, though I have included, to the right, just the first page of the notes on my journey as an example.

Forgiveness and Release

My reflection on my early childhood and adolescent years enabled me to realize I was harboring built-up stress and anger from those years that I needed to release. I needed to forgive those involved and myself for some things that occurred. At the very least I needed to release the hold that some of those past events had on me. I had to begin devoting my energy to living in the present and creating my future in the here and now.

Through the process of watching past events as a movie, as a detached observer rather than as a participant, I was able to release the hold these

My Journey

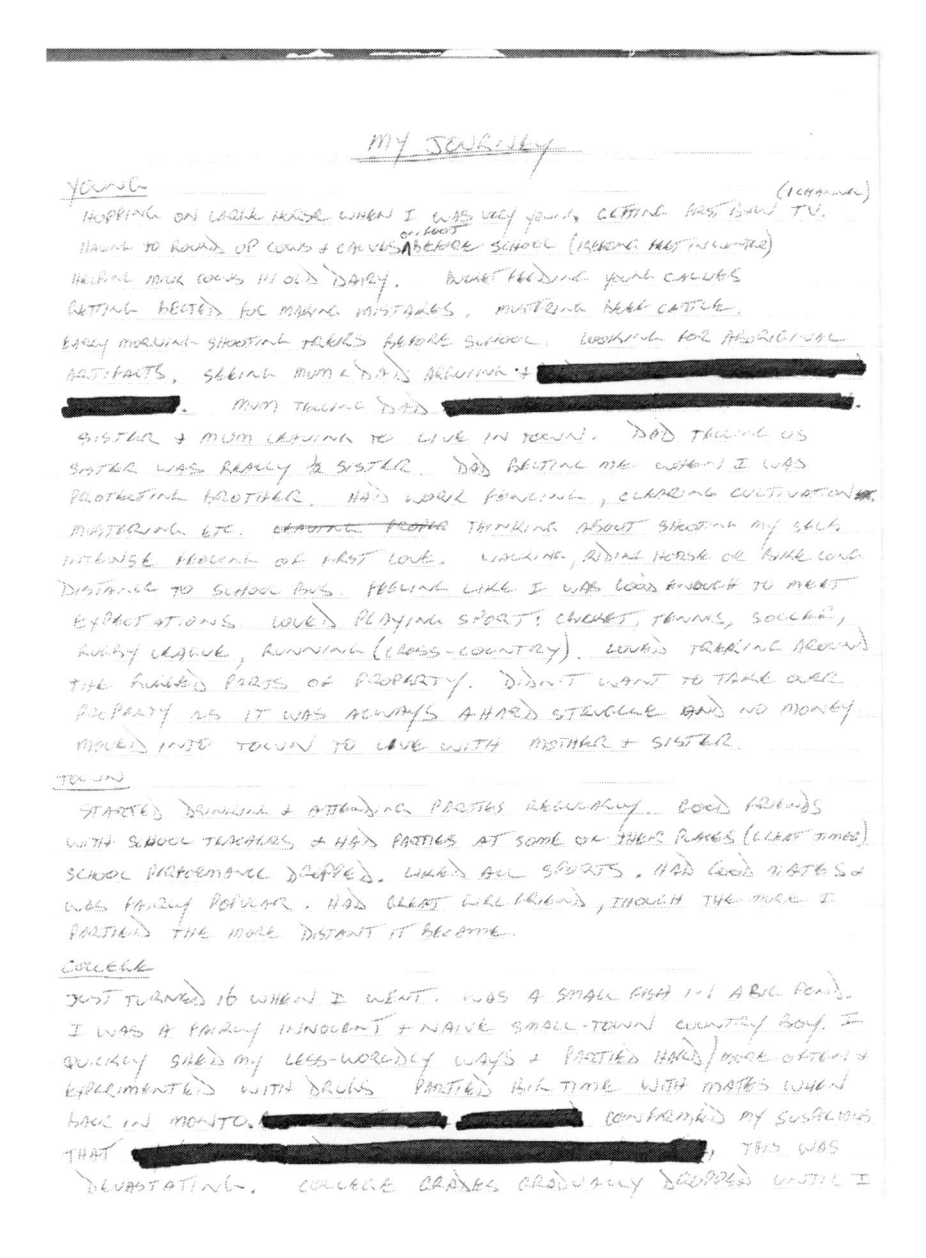

Young
(1 chapter)
Hopping on wooden horse when I was very young. Getting first black & white TV. Having to round up cows & calves before/after school (riding horse/motorbike). Helping milk cows at old dairy. Bucket feeding young calves. Getting belted for making mistakes. Mustering herd cattle. Early morning shooting rabbits before school. Looking for Aboriginal artifacts. Seeing mum & dad arguing + ▓▓▓▓▓▓. Mum hitting dad ▓▓▓▓▓▓. Sister & mum leaving to live in town. Dad telling us sister was really ½ sister. Dad belting me when I was protecting brother. Hard work fencing, clearing, cultivating, mustering etc. Thinking about shooting my self. Intense feelings of first love. Walking, riding horse or bike long distance to school bus. Feeling like I was good enough to meet expectations. Loved playing sports; cricket, tennis, soccer, rugby league, running (cross-country). Loved trekking around the hundred parts of property. Didn't want to take over property as it was always a hard struggle and no money. Moved into town to live with mother & sister.

Town
Started drinking & attending parties regularly. Good friends with school teachers, & had parties at some of their places (great times). School performance dropped. Liked all sports. Had good mates & was fairly popular. Had great girlfriends, though the more I partied the more distant it became.

College
Just turned 16 when I went. Was a small fish in a big pond. I was a fairly innocent & naïve small-town country boy. I quickly shed my less-worldly ways & partied hard/more often & experimented with drugs. Partied all time with mates when back in Monto. ▓▓▓▓▓▓▓▓▓▓ confirmed my suspicions that ▓▓▓▓▓▓▓▓▓▓▓▓▓▓▓▓▓▓▓▓▓▓, this was devastating. College grades gradually dropped until I

events had over me and start to forgive those involved. This included forgiving myself for some of the things I was not proud of. Don't be mistaken: forgiveness doesn't mean condoning or validating things that you believe are intrinsically wrong. It is more about you releasing the hold that they have had on you since they happened. An understanding of why someone has done a harmful act doesn't make it right. You have to realize that the fault lies with the transgressor, and your integrity, values, self-worth and power should remain intact. Understanding each incident and releasing any grip it has on you is the key to forgiveness. The memories aren't erased and can still be unpleasant to recall, though I now look at them in a different light, with an understanding of why they occurred, and they no longer have any hold over me.

A huge help in the process of forgiveness of others (and yourself) is the comprehension that most people are simply behaving in a way that corresponds to their level of awareness and personal growth at that time. It is how they themselves were taught and conditioned, or what they determined was the best way based on their ignorance and underdeveloped reasoning ability. At worst, for lack of knowing any better way, out of frustration or anger they may have drawn on some (now inappropriate) primal instinct, resulting in aggressive behavior.

By going back and reflecting on your younger years you can reassess how you lived and what you learned and now make better-informed decisions on what to keep and what to change. An important part of this process is forgiving those—including ourselves—for poor actions and choices made, when at the time they—or you—didn't know a better way.[9]

I can vividly remember a time when I had a huge release of emotional baggage that had obviously had built up since I was a child. It was so momentous that it shocked me and everyone else present who witnessed it, as up to that point in my life I had learned to have a fairly tight rein on my internal emotions and what I showed externally. I'd had a fair few drinks at a friend's dinner party and was later sitting outside by myself contemplating my childhood days and circumstances. When trying to recall some pleasant memories and forgiving some unpleasant ones from those days, a completely uncontrollable surge of emotional energy welled up from my inner depths. I couldn't help but to start to cry uncontrollably, to the extent that the other guests came to see what the matter was. At the time it was very embarrassing for me, though is a prime example of how powerful these releases of holds from the past can be. I had been letting

---

9   For more resources on forgiveness, visit www.alcohemy.com.

past and present external circumstances dictate my internal happiness and success in life, and that was not acceptable. I knew I could do so much more if I'd just let go of my past, get off my arse, and put some real focus and commitment into being the best I could be. I was facing and grieving the fact that I had let myself be a victim of my past and over the years had chosen to seek comfort and pleasure in varying degrees from alcohol, sex, and drugs.

We all are subject to challenging events, circumstances, and experiences in life that are outside of our control. Some of these can leave us feeling quite powerless. It is very important to realize that it is our choice whether we become a long-term victim of the event or circumstance, or whether we retain our own righteous power and self-worth. You are the only person in control of your thoughts, feelings, and actions; therefore, your future is in your control unless you choose to give it away.

I had formed my identity and character around my early circumstances and had locked myself in to that way of life. My emotional lifeometer was giving me readings that I was not on track with my real desires, and I had been enhancing my pleasure levels with alcohol and other external means. I had confined and bound myself to lamenting the past and made myself a victim by using alcohol as false means of feeling good. The sense and conscious acknowledgment that I was letting myself down by not being more than I was at the time had become a major issue for me, and that frustration was also being felt in this uncontrolled flood of emotion.

Passions and Positive Events: The Seed of the True Self

During your reflection on your life history, also be sure to note some of the particularly positive aspects and passions you had as well the low points. These very happy occasions and passions will be indicators of the types of things you could again incorporate into your life to produce a more fulfilling and happy experience. Quite often our childhood and adolescent passions are dismissed and left behind when we reach adulthood, as we are taught to stop fantasizing and to focus more on settling for a "real" or "standard" job, most often a job designed to meet our predicted financial needs but not our emotional or creative needs. This in turn can lead to dissatisfaction, frustration, and a sense of nonfulfillment, tempting people to use artificial, harmful means such as alcohol and drugs in pursuit of an internal sense of feeling better. Rekindling past passions and creative desires and incorporating those into your current work or social situations can help boost fading contentment. In my youth I had a fire and passion for creativity, adventure, and discovery burning inside me that was left unfulfilled. Though I had unsuccessfully tried many things over the years to express that creative and adventurous passion (hard work, mustering, hunting, sex, drugs, alcohol, etc.), the unfulfilled desire never left me. It always remained an intrinsic part of me waiting to be expressed. If you spend some quality time reflecting on what did or would make you truly happy, I'm sure you will find a passion or two of yours still waiting to be released and fulfilled. Consider rekindling these to replace your negative substance habit.

Assignment: Element 1

Go to the Element 1 worksheet of your Element Workbook (see the appendix for sample forms, or download a free copy at www.alcohemy.com) and record your significant emotional events as a child and through to present time.

Some questions to consider for Element 1:

1. What were your main joys and passions?
2. What made you frustrated or triggered negative emotions?
3. What incidents did you have difficulty dealing with and perhaps suppressed or left unresolved?
4. What do you need to forgive yourself for and let go of?
5. What do you need to forgive others for and let go of?
6. What past events are you using to support a victim mentality?
7. What are some of the earliest memories you have of others consuming alcohol?
8. What are some of the earliest memories you have of you consuming alcohol and why?

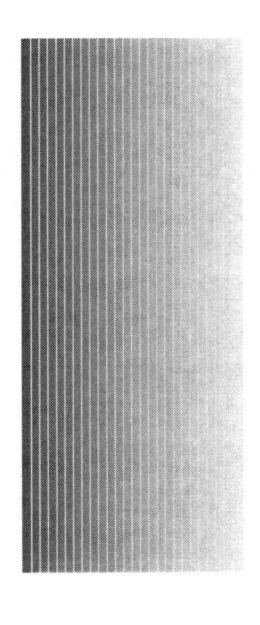

ELEMENT 2

Record Your Associations with Alcohol

Also hidden in the mass of the alcohol habit weed roots are your early associations with alcohol use. These introductions may have been very prominent or quite subtle in nature. Either way, our young impressionable minds readily accepted the advice and examples set by people we know and trust in our circle of influence. These strong influences are usually family, friends, people you admire in the community, social media, and cleverly crafted advertising designed to make young people believe they will be better off by using a certain product or behaving in a certain way. At a very young age we don't have the comprehension or experience to rationally determine that alcohol use has the potential to have a major negative impact on our life. I suggest that usually young children see alcohol use as something that adds fun and happiness to social occasions and is also consumed to help relax after a day's work. It is perceived as an adult or mature thing to do, and most young kids can't wait to be considered mature or adult. All these perceived benefits add to the why you wanted to start drinking.

Another one of the reasons for your journey back in time is to take note of the very early and adolescent memories and associations you had with alcohol. At the time they may not have been strikingly conscious opinions you formed, though now with the benefit of hindsight and adult reasoning you may see what actual influence those associations had on your young mind. To keep a record for your review and analysis, these early alcohol associations should be recorded in a table format. Below I have shown what my original rough notes looked like, as an example.

Occasion	Belief/Lesson	Positive Impression?	Issues? with Values
CFC Nights	Fun/Relax/Adult	Yes	No
Kitchen – Taste	Taste Bad	No	Yes
BBQs	Fun/Relax/Adult	Yes	No
Dances	"	Mostly	Yes
TV Ads	" / Popular	Yes	No
Auction	Adult / mostly	Mostly	No
Girlfriend's Place	Fun/Relax/Adult	Yes	No
Smith's Shed Hideout	Not Allowed / Adult	Yes	Yes
Teacher's House	"	Mostly	Yes
College Life	Fun / with consequences	Mostly	Yes
Bike Crash	Too much / Serious consequences	No	Yes
Rodeo Fight	" / "	No	Yes
Steal Alcohol	Bad choices	No	Yes
Brisbane Life	Fun / with consequences	Not always	Yes
Early H/Bay Life	"	Not always	Yes
Early Married Life	"	"	Yes
Mid → Now Married Life	Lost control / Not happy!	Mostly not	Yes

The "Event/Occasion" column is where you list all the very early memories and significant later events you have regarding alcohol. The "Belief/Lesson" column is to note what belief you adopted from the lesson you learned from those occasions. The "Positive Impression?" column is designed to get you to think about whether those occasions were at the time viewed as favorable and left a good impression. In hindsight they may now seem inappropriate, though it is what you thought at the time that helped formed your beliefs. You will most likely (as I did) find your early associations with alcohol as favorable and more recent ones as not. *Don't fill in the "Conflict with Values?" column until Element 3, after Element 2 is completed.* It is designed to check if the key associations you had then and more recently align with your current values. This can help you change belief from what may have been a positive reinforcement back then to a more appropriate belief that serves you better now. Being aware of what motivated you then and what is now more appropriate is a big factor in accepting and driving change.

Assignment: Element 2

Go to the Element 2 worksheet of your Element Workbook and record your associations with alcohol, considering the beliefs and lessons you learned from these associations and whether they now serve you and match your core values. In particular, consider the following:

1. List the earliest memories you have of others and yourself consuming alcohol followed by the other significant alcohol events from young adulthood to present time, in the "Event/Occasion" column.
2. Consider these carefully and record in the "Belief/Lesson" column what you believe they meant to you at the time they happened.
3. Record in the "Positive Impression?" column whether at the time of the event you would have formed a positive view of it.
4. Do *not* fill in the "Conflict with Values?" column at this stage. You will do that later as part of Element 3.

ELEMENT 3

Record Your Life Values

After you have taken your intimate journey from your earliest memories through to your current life, it is an appropriate time to consider and document what your core values are, where you believe they originated from, and whether they are still values you wish to uphold now. Values in this case are your moral principles and beliefs or accepted moral standards of behavior. For example, how do you respect and treat other people? Is using good manners and being polite important to you? How important is being honest, fair, or helpful to others? What kind of work ethic do you have, and why? If some of what you were originally taught or conditioned to value is not now valid or appropriate to your current desires, consider this: What do you now value instead of those things? This is critical in driving the internal changes you need to make to become truly free from undesirable habits.

Often when we think or do things that are in conflict with our current deeper values, we experience discord, inner anxiety, and turmoil. Our lifeometer registers at the negative and unhappy end of the emotional scale, warning us that our life is off track. These profound feelings of misalignment are a source of emotional stress that can also feed the alcohol habit weed by giving a false justification to a decision to drink to feel better. Here is a copy of my original personal notes on this point.

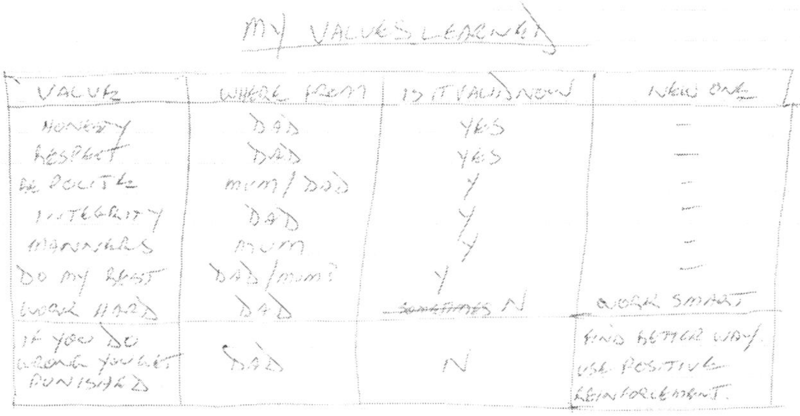

[Handwritten notes: "MY VALUES LEARNED"]

VALUE	WHERE FROM	IS IT VALID NOW	NEW ONE
Honesty	Dad	Yes	—
Respect	Dad	Yes	—
Be Polite	Mum / Dad	Y	—
Integrity	Dad	Y	—
Manners	Mum	Y	—
Do my Best	Dad / Mum	Y	—
Work Hard	Dad	Sometimes N	Work Smart
If you do what you like, punished	Dad	N	Find better way. Use positive reinforcement.

On the Element 3 worksheet of the Element Workbook, the "What Values Did I Learn Back Then?" column is for you to list all the values you believe you had when younger and ones you hold dear now. The "From Where or from Whom Did I Get Them?" column is to list where you believe you got this value from. It most likely will be a family member or close relative, though it might be from respected friends, TV, or social media. The "Are They Still Valid Now?" column is for you to decide whether this value is applicable to how you would like to live your life now and into the future. Some older and embedded values may not serve you now that you desire to live a better life. For example, you may have been raised and conditioned when young to be intolerant of a race other than your own. Now that you are older and understand that this is not appropriate or supportive of leading a successful and happy personal and business life, this needs to change.

The "If No, What Value Has Replaced It?" column is where you can list what new values you have chosen to replace any obsolete ones. In the example above, a replacement value would be to treat and value all people equally regardless of race, skin color, gender, sexuality, or religious belief. Instead, you might form your opinion of others based on their genuine nature and character and value they add to those around them.

After you have completed Element 3, go back to the Element 2 table and consider if any of the beliefs and lessons you learned when younger now conflict with your confirmed current values. Note these in the "Conflict with Values?" column in Element 2.

Assignment: Element 3

Go to the Element 3 worksheet of your Element Workbook and record your answers to the following questions:

1. Reflect on and list in the "What Values…" column what principles, moral standards, and values you either were conditioned with when young or have come to hold dear since from your own reasoning.
2. Consider where you learned that value from and record it in the "From Where…" column.
3. Record in the "Are They Still Valid Now?" column if your beliefs about those values listed support your current desires and the success you would like to have in all areas of your life.
4. If you have identified some old values that aren't appropriate now, consider replacement values and record them in the "…Replaced It?" column.

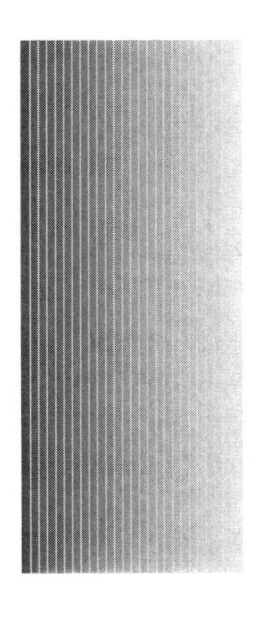

ELEMENT 4

RECORD WHAT ALCOHOL DOES FOR YOU

Now we will identify the thoughts and beliefs governing your justification of why you continue to habitually drink and the benefits you believe alcohol provides. Before you begin considering the reasons why you currently drink, I'd like to explain the deeper principles of why I believe most people consume alcohol and the reasons they should not.

Apart from purely ritualistic or symbolic occasions and infrequent "for taste only" experiences, I believe every reason we drink alcohol (or take any mind-altering substance, for that matter) can be reduced to the core reason of simply wanting to feel better internally than how we currently feel. Regardless of whether we are feeling okay or are trying to block some unpleasant memory, we are somehow trying to feel better or happier than we currently do.

The irony, though, is that alcohol is a sensory depressant, so by consuming it we actually 'feel' less. Some may dispute this statement by recalling times when they or others have seemed to show increased emotions after consuming alcohol. The fact is that our awareness of stimuli from the environment around us is reduced, as is our cognitive ability to process internal emotions. It is not that we start experiencing more or heightened emotions after consuming alcohol; rather, our ability to suppress or control the ones we already have is greatly reduced. What we kept concealed before due to social protocols or public expectations begin to surface when we drink by way of behaviors we wouldn't consciously show when sober.

That is the reason why people who are genuinely very satisfied and happy at a deep core level when sober get visibly emotionally happy and loving when drunk. At the same time, people who harbor deep emotions of discontentment, resentment, anger, low self-esteem, or emotional baggage from the past can become very mean, sarcastic, sad, angry, or aggressive as those emotions become unsuppressed, bubble to the surface, and are displayed in an unrestrained manner.

I know this only too well, as many times when intoxicated if a conversation or my personal thoughts triggered some negative baggage I was harboring, my demeanor could become depressive or unpleasant. Moreover, the simple frustration of knowing that I had an alcohol dependency I could not control and that I was not being the person I could be was enough to trigger a miserable and negative mood when affected by alcohol.

Ideally most of us want everything in our lives to be a positive experience all the time. "Well, why not?" I imagine a lot of you will ask, as that is a reasonable question. I believe the problem lies in our perception of how we view the experiences that happen to us and around us. We tend to want to place all our experiences in either a "good stuff" or "bad stuff" box, and perhaps we have a "not really sure" box as well. To us, anything in the bad stuff box is unpleasant and unacceptable, therefore we don't like having to deal with this stuff.

If we perceive it is unpleasant enough or happens often enough, it is culturally acceptable in a lot of countries to self-medicate with alcohol or other drugs simply to mask or change how we are feeling about that stuff. We see ourselves as a victim of some bad circumstance and we need to cure ourselves of the symptoms (change our feelings) or pretend it isn't happening (block our feelings).

The problem with changing or blocking negative feelings about certain experiences is that we miss the whole point of having feelings about our experiences in the first place. We are meant to feel every sensation of every experience we have, positive or negative or somewhere in between. These feelings are meant to last for whatever time is necessary for us to learn from them and accept that they are now part of who we are. Feelings and emotions are the measures on our lifeometer gauge and let us know how aligned our thoughts and actions are with our values and desires.

Most people tend to believe everything in this world is made up of opposites or opposing forces, as if they were two completely different things: black/white, up/down, in/out, heads/tails, hot/cold, right/wrong, good/bad. In fact, it is only our human perception that puts an experience into one category or the other based on what we are comparing it to. These opposites are just different points on the same thing and neither point could exist without the other to compare it to. For example, you can't have an up without a down to compare it to, because both are just describing a place in space. The same applies to in and out; one can't exist without the other. There can be no 'heads' side of a coin without a 'tails' side as they are just two necessary places on the same coin; hot and cold are just subjective descriptions based on our human perception of the one thing called temperature, and there can't be one without the other's existence. Similarly, there is no right or good without our perception of what a wrong or bad is.

By viewing most emotional opposites (dichotomies) as mutually exclusive, or intrinsically either good or bad, we tend to fear and loathe experiencing what we perceive as bad. By not recognizing that you need to experience both ends of the scale to understand the fullness of our life experience, we miss the opportunity to learn more about ourselves and grow both mentally and spiritually. We cannot fully appreciate the great joys in life if we have not also experienced the great sorrows. We learn more about ourselves from when we believe we are going through our darkest hours than we ever will when things are going great. In fact, it is these times that are usually the most defining moments in our lives and bring about our greatest advancements in knowledge and character. We should never hide from and avoid these experiences, like so many of us have by using alcohol or drugs to deliberately alter our experience of life. We should allow ourselves to engage in the experience and try to view it as something that is necessary for our soul's growth and to fully appreciate both ends of the emotional spectrum.

Just like great businesspeople and athletes have had to endure the physical and mental pain, endurance, and heartache of hard training and setbacks on the way to great success, so do we all on life's journey. The difference between the average and the great achievers in life is that the great achievers accept they are going to experience significant challenges and setbacks along the way, and they use these experiences to better understand themselves and develop their skills. They recognize that challenges are part of the bigger process and choose to view them differently from the average person. The people who achieve great success understand that challenge and success are part of the same process, and they will experience greater reward *because of* the challenges they experience, not in spite of them.

To fully appreciate the richness of life, we need to experience a large range of circumstances, regardless of whether we would have typically put them in our good stuff or bad stuff boxes, and embrace these as part of the whole, or the big box we call life. This might be hard for those who have experienced significant grief to accept, like those who have gone through a tough relationship breakup or the death of a loved one. Even these occasions are intrinsically neither good nor bad, except for the value we place on them. There are cultures that celebrate the death of a person and their passing into a better afterlife as much as they celebrate their birth into this world. They are each considered part of a greater "one thing," and it is only our perception that makes them appear to be different. A relationship breakup is part of a whole relationship experience, and any sadness about the breakup would not be possible without the joy of the relationship beginning. The great sadness at the death of a loved one at the end of their earthly life cycle could not be possible without the great joy of that person's birth and knowing them while they were alive. You can't experience one aspect without the other, so we need to accept and fully experience all parts of the whole. Every human life must have an earthly beginning and end, as do all relationships. I believe that everything that we experience in life is designed to serve us in some way.

It is with the preceding comments in mind that I emphasize we are doing ourselves and others a great injustice by using alcohol or other means to filter out, avoid, or mask the feelings associated with any of the bad stuff. We need to sense and feel all aspects of events and situations as they are presented and try to see them all as different versions of good stuff. When you take a big box perspective on things, the saying "it's all good" really does have validity.

Our emotions function as our intellectual and spiritual guidance system (our personal lifeometer), which we learn from and use in making choices about how we wish our lives to progress. To best do this we need to fully feel and appreciate what we perceive to be the highs of the mountains and the depths of the valleys. Our innate desires along with these emotional experiences help calibrate our lifeometer and give us feedback as to whether we are on our true path or not. When we are feeling unpleasant feelings, perceived stress, or any negative emotion we associate with the lower end of our lifeometer, it is likely that our actions and definitely our thoughts are not in alignment with our intended desires, and we need to change them.

This is why using alcohol (or drugs) to avoid or mask this emotional feedback is counterproductive to achieving our desired success. It would be like tampering with the thermometer in a refrigerator in a way such that it was always registering that it was sufficiently cold, regardless of the actual internal temperature. No matter how warm it was actually getting, the inboard computer would always believe the refrigerator was cold enough and not start its cooling action. Very soon all the food would spoil and go rotten. Similarly, if you tamper with your emotional lifeometer (with alcohol/drugs) to deal with stress and to fool yourself into believing you are feeling better than you really are, then you are not likely to take any action to change the reality. As with the fridge analogy, without realistic emotional feedback, you will not change to more appropriate thoughts and actions, therefore your mind and results will continue to "spoil" and remain unsatisfactory.

The reality is that there is no objective experience we could label as stress. Whatever stress we experience, we create ourselves through our own perception. What we commonly term stress is merely the result of placing our own negative perception on an occurrence. An occurrence that one person of a particular upbringing, religion, gender, culture, or level of enlightenment might perceive as very stressful could to another seem quite reasonable and a natural part of life's valuable feedback.

A very useful technique to adopt when starting to feel stressed is to really examine why you are feeling the way you are about the event. Question whether you can look at it from another angle to find some good in it. Remember, what we perceive as good stuff and bad stuff is all part of the same single thing called life, and you cannot have one without the other. If we can perceive something bad about an event, then there also must be something good to be found in that same thing. It usually is not apparent to us because we are so focused on our negative perceptions. We just have to remove the filter that looks for the bad and exchange it for one that looks for the good. When you change the way you look at things, the things you look at change. If you look for and find the good in everything, regardless of first impressions, what we perceive as stress is alleviated and the temptation to use alcohol to deal with it is reduced.[10]

With all that in mind, I'd like to invite you to begin considering what reasons you have for consuming alcohol and the benefits it provides. When reflecting on the perceived benefits, be sure to consider whether your alcohol or other dependency falls into the category of what I call an 'advantageous disadvantage'. This is where you use a known disadvantage (such as an alcohol habit) as a phony advantage (i.e., an excuse not to attempt to do something you probably should). Removing the disadvantage (the alcohol

---

10 One excellent example that illustrates how our minds filter for things we are expecting to happen and filter out a lot of other information is the Gorilla in the Midst experiment, which can be viewed at www.theinvisiblegorilla.com.

habit) and therefore your excuse (a phony advantage) could leave you feeling insecure, incompetent, challenged, and even fearful of endeavoring to be all you can be.

An example of this is when people use physical or psychosomatic illnesses and disabilities as excuses not to do things that involve getting out of their comfort zone. They can also play the sympathy card to avoid doing things they don't like, or gain an unfair advantage in things they do like. Of course there are legitimate reasons people with genuine disabilities should be given special consideration, and many in that category leave able-bodied people for dead when it comes to striving to be the best they can. What I am suggesting is that many people capable of doing more with their lives choose not to, and they use all sorts of excuses to mask their apathy or fear of failure. They would rather adopt a victim role than risk looking incompetent or like a failure in the eyes of others.

I know I used to think things like, *If I hadn't developed an early dependency to alcohol, I would have been way more successful than I am now*, and *Drinking alcohol is a part of who I am now, so it's too late for me to change*, or *I can't do what I need to do to be more successful because it's not compatible with my drinking habit*. I had let myself develop a victim mentality regarding my habit. By knowing that an alcohol dependency is a distinct disadvantage to being successful in many personal and business endeavors, I gained the advantage of using it as an excuse to not commit to significant effort. Also, when I believed the general public opinion that an alcohol addiction is a lifetime illness, I had an excuse to not even consider ceasing altogether, let alone dedicate substantial mental and physical energy to it.

In my case, my alcohol habit served as an advantageous disadvantage in that it allowed me to let myself off the hook for not being more of a success and for settling for average results personally and financially. I mean, how could anyone be expected to be out there putting in the necessary 100 percent commitment if they had a significant alcohol dependence . . . right? Below you'll see my notes on the benefits I felt I received from alcohol.

128 | ALCOHEMY

[Handwritten worksheet: "WHAT DO I GET FROM ALCOHOL"]

BENEFITS
1. Helps me relax
2. Problems seem less important
3. I feel more confident
4. Get a warm buzz
5. Being "addicted" to alcohol gives me reason for not being more successful

NEGATIVE IMPACTS
1. Affects my decision making ability
2. Slows down & slurs my speech
3. Reduces my memory retention
4. Feel tired next day
5. I think over a lot next day
6. Get dehydrated / dry skin
7. My moods get exaggerated
8. My balance gets affected
9. Others get a poor impression of me
10. Once I start I have trouble stopping
11. Loss of appetite when drinking
12. Gain body fat
13. Decrease in fitness
14. Decreased motivation to train
15. Can't drive
16. Set bad example to sons
17. Increase family tension
18. Don't think clearly/rationally
19. Poor body health re: liver, kidneys, intestines

Looking back at your past and current habit, in the "Perceived Benefits of Alcohol" column on the Element 4 worksheet, list *all* the particular reasons you used to (and still do) believe you benefit from drinking alcohol (your current whys). If you spend some time thinking about it, you will be surprised at just how many reasons (or excuses) you have for regular or excessive drinking. If by reading this book you have experienced a shift in the way you think about alcohol, please still list what you used to believe were the benefits.

In addition to the benefits you believe you get, list in the "Perceived Negative Impacts of Alcohol" column all the harmful or undesirable side effects and consequences you also get from alcohol use. These form the basis of why you should cease. Spend some time and be totally honest with yourself. List as many as you can think of in both columns. All of these will help you compare and assess your logic and reasoning later in Elements 7.

Assignment: Element 4

Go to the Element 4 worksheet of the Element Workbook and record your answers to the following questions:

1. Consider all the reasons why you like to consume alcoholic drinks. What advantages do you believe you get from alcohol? List these in the "Perceived Benefits of Alcohol" column.
2. Consider all the issues or disadvantages you know or believe alcohol consumption causes you and list these in the "Perceived Negative Impacts of Alcohol" column. Remember things that may not be visibly obvious, like health, finance, relationships, self-esteem, business performance, reputation, motivation, and so on.

ELEMENT 5

RECORD THE EFFECTS OF CEASING YOUR HABIT

Some people are motivated to move toward conditions and rewards they find very desirable, while others are more motivated to move away from conditions and situations that they don't want to have in their life. More often, though, it is a combination of both that drives people to make significant changes. It is important to list both the positive effects of ceasing your alcohol consumption and the negative effects of continuing your drinking habit. Quite often we consider only the consequences and effects that are immediately apparent after each undesirable alcohol-related incident, though when we take the time to reflect back on them, collectively the consequences can be far-reaching. Again, spend some time on these, and be totally honest with yourself. This element and the next two elements will help you examine the effects of both ceasing alcohol and not ceasing alcohol from different angles so no stone is left unturned. As a result, these exercises will further reveal the reasons you currently drink and reasons why you should cease. Although these elements require less explanation than the others, they are no less important.

In particular, Element 5 examines what you think would happen to you and the people around you if you permanently stopped drinking alcohol. Think of it as if you could flick a switch and you were suddenly alcohol-free without any withdrawal symptoms or cravings. How do you believe this would this affect you in both positive and negative ways?

It was fairly easy for me to find the benefits of ceasing alcohol consumption. I just had to look at all the negative things that alcohol caused in my life and imagine what my happiness would be like without them. Examining what I believed were some negative impacts of me not drinking involved contemplating what perceived benefits I would miss out on, as well as some of my fears and concerns of the unknown. Two of my biggest concerns were what would I do with myself during the times I would normally be drinking (either at home or socially), and what would all my friends and acquaintances think of me being a teetotaler. I would have to deal with all the questions from people and explain why I was taking this course of action. This would surely lead them to knowing I have a problem with alcohol and that would be very embarrassing and distressing for me. However, as part of my overall Alcohemy strategy, I planned in advance to deal with these fears, as you will see in Elements 8 and 10. First, though, I needed to identify what disadvantages I believed I would experience by stopping drinking, as well as the obvious advantages.

Below are my own notes on how I believed my life would change if I could instantly cease drinking alcohol, both the positives and negatives.

EFFECTS OF STOPPING

BENEFITS of STOPPING	ANY NEGATIVES of STOPPING
- NO MORE EMBARRASSING TIMES WHEN FROM DRINKING - BETTER RELATIONSHIP WITH FAMILY - " " " FRIENDS - NO MEMORY BLACKOUTS - NO HANGOVERS - NOT TIRED EVERY MORNING - BETTER LONG-TERM HEALTH - MORE ENERGY + MOTIVATION - CAN DRIVE ANY TIME - GREATER SELF-ESTEEM - SAVE LOTS OF MONEY - MY DECISION MAKING WILL BE BETTER - WILL DO MORE THING TO ADVANCE PERSONALLY + BUSINESS	- HAVE TO FIND SOMETHING TO REPLACE DRINKING ALCOHOL - HAVE TO DEAL WITH QUESTIONS FROM OTHERS

Assignment: Element 5

Go to the Element 5 worksheet of your Element Workbook and record your answers to the following:

1. In the "Perceived Benefits of Ceasing Alcohol" column list the all the positive aspects and possible improvements in your life if you were completely free from alcohol.
2. In the "Perceived Negatives of Ceasing Alcohol" column list the disadvantages you believe would occur for you if you were completely alcohol-free.

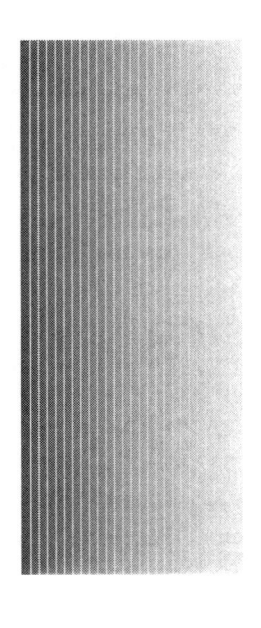

ELEMENT 6

RECORD THE EFFECTS OF *NOT* CEASING YOUR HABIT

This may appear to some to be a duplication of Element 5, except with an opposite tack. I included it because when you look at things from the opposite viewpoint, you become aware of thoughts and realizations that you may not have considered earlier. Not everyone's mind rationalizes the same way, and I want to make sure you capture all the pros and cons of discontinuing or continuing your alcohol habit.

Don't be concerned if your answers are similar to those in Element 5; write them down in the appropriate columns anyway. This element is designed to keep probing your mind and reveal any additional reasons you may have. Rest assured that if you don't fully complete the mental part of this Alcohemy process, you will not change the way you feel about using alcohol, and the results may not be permanent. You may get all the way through Element 13, set your start date, and even get

134 | ALCOHEMY

weeks into ceasing, but sooner or later when you are put under pressure and it is convenient to use alcohol to feel better, you may fall back into old ways. The mental preparation part of this process is designed to change the way you view using alcohol at a core level, shifting from the viewpoint of "it helps me and makes me happy" to the realization that drinking alcohol only has negative consequences. There is not one thing alcohol can do for you that you can't achieve yourself by other healthy means.

Below are my notes on the effects of not stopping my alcohol habit.

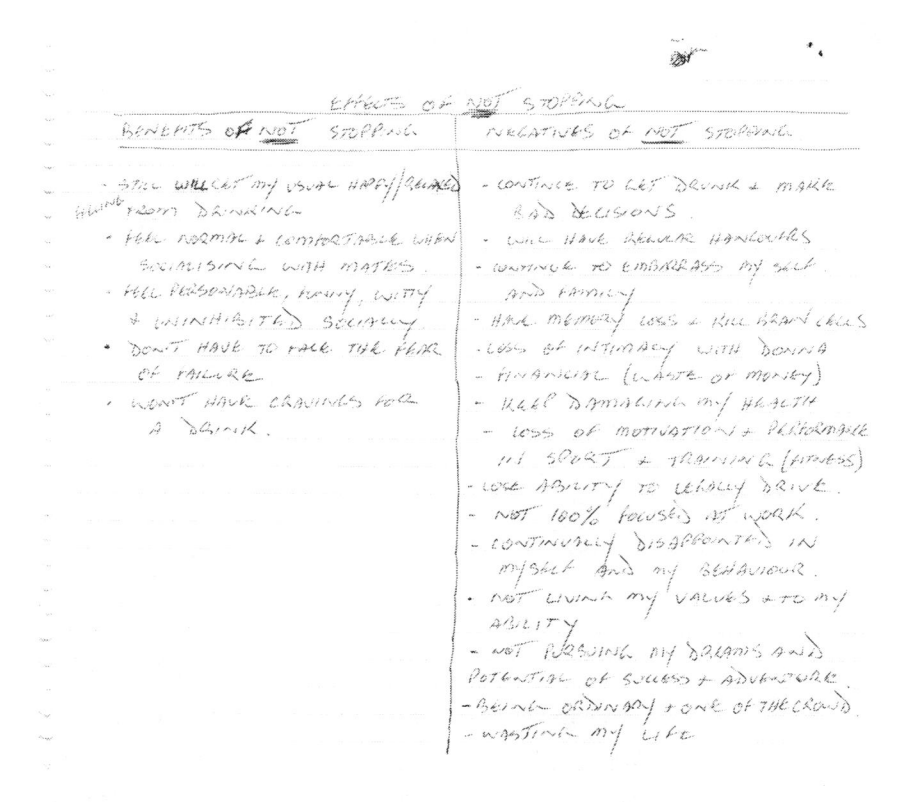

[Handwritten notes: Effects of Not Stopping]

Benefits of not stopping:
- Still will get my usual happy/buzzed feeling from drinking
- Feel normal & comfortable when socialising with mates
- Feel personable, funny, witty & uninhibited socially
- Don't have to face the fear of failure
- Won't have cravings for a drink

Negatives of not stopping:
- Continue to get drunk & make bad decisions
- Will have regular hangovers
- Continue to embarrass myself and family
- Have memory loss & kill brain cells
- Loss of intimacy with Donna
- Financial (waste of money)
- Keep damaging my health
- Loss of motivation & performance in sport & training (fitness)
- Lose ability to legally drive
- Not 100% focused at work
- Continually disappointed in myself and my behaviour
- Not living my values & to my ability
- Not pursuing my dreams and potential of success & adventure
- Being ordinary & one of the crowd
- Wasting my life

Assignment: Element 6

Go to the Element 6 worksheet of your Element Workbook and record your answers to the following:

Record the Effects of Not Ceasing Your Habit

1. In the "Perceived Benefits of *Not* Ceasing Alcohol" column, list the real benefits you would maintain if you kept your alcohol habit.
2. In the "Perceived Negatives of *Not* Ceasing Alcohol" column, list all issues and disadvantages you could experience if you kept your alcohol habit.

ELEMENT 7

RECORD THE COMPILATION OF TOTAL EFFECTS OF CONSUMING ALCOHOL VERSUS CURRENT VALUES

In this element, you will be able to gain a complete view of the combined perceived benefits and actual disadvantages you get from your habit of drinking alcohol. It is a combination of the lists you made in the last three elements (Elements 4, 5, and 6). By listing all my reasoning in one 'pros and cons' table, I was clearly able to see the overwhelming evidence for ceasing my alcohol habit. You can see from my list at the end of this section I had recorded a combined total of thirty-four reasons *why* I should cease drinking. It would defy common sense and logic not to dedicate 100 percent effort to finally achieving an alcohol-free status. To see all this evidence visibly presented was very important in helping me make the resolute decision and commitment to start and see the process through to the end, no matter what it took.

The great achievers in life, recognized and admired by many, are people with the same ability as you and me to make firm decisions and resolute commitments. The reason they are acclaimed is that they have chosen very worthy and challenging goals and were prepared to do whatever it took to be successful. They formed very strong personal 'whys' to fuel their commitment and rev their motivational engine. They were prepared to step out of their comfort zone, altered the way they thought about the goal, and developed a success attitude.

This is what you must do. Look at all the reasons you have written why *you* should be alcohol-free. Note the big ones that will rev your engine and make the definite decision to do it. Then commit 100 percent to doing everything necessary to achieve your new rewarding life. I found that in the past just looking at each individual negative impact on its own (as they periodically occurred) wasn't effective, because that way it was much easier to make individual excuses for my behavior. This would diminish my perception of the overall effect my habit had on my past and present health, wealth, and happiness, as well as on others in my total area of influence. I suggest you print and place this combined list somewhere you can see it every day to remind yourself why you are committed to this significant, positive change to your life. Remember, if you find yourself a powerful enough why, and combine it with the belief that it is possible to do it, then there will be nothing you can't do. You will be the master of your fate and the captain of your soul.

Also, by noting if these benefits and disadvantages align with your current values, you can confirm if it is a result that is still valid and you wish to keep. If you have noted that a perceived benefit of using alcohol has a valid current value aligned with it, there will be other healthy alternatives available to achieve the same result. For example, perhaps one of your perceived benefits of drinking alcohol is that you believe it gives you more confidence at social occasions. Having social confidence may be a valid result and align with your values, but there are far healthier ways of raising your level of confidence and self-esteem than using alcohol. You need to note these and actively pursue these healthy, life-enhancing alternatives. Element 10 and its associated exercise will help reveal new actions to replace old harmful ones.

See my compilation of effects listed on the next page.

COMPILATION OF EFFECTS

COMBINED BENEFITS OF STOPPING	VALUE	PERCEIVED REASONS TO DRINK	VALUE
1) BETTER DECISION MAKING ABILITY	Y	1) HELPS ME RELAX (EXTRINSIC)	N
2) NO SLURRED OR SLOW SPEECH	Y	2) PROBLEMS SEEM LESS IMPORTANT	N
3) BETTER MEMORY RETENTION (SHORT & LONG TERM)	Y	3) FEEL MORE CONFIDENT (ARTIFICIAL)	N
4) WON'T BE TIRED NEXT DAY	Y	4) GET A WARM BUZZ (ARTIFICIAL)	N
5) " " HUNGOVER OR SICK	Y	5) EXCUSE NOT TO BE SUCCESSFUL	N
6) " " DEHYDRATED	Y	6) WON'T HAVE TO FACE FEAR OF FAILURE	N
7) " HAVE EXAGGERATED MOODS	Y		
8) " BE UNCOORDINATED OR STUMBLE	Y	7) WILL FIT IN WITH MY MATES	N
9) " CREATE BAD IMPRESSIONS BY BEING DRUNK	Y	8) WON'T GET PROBING QUESTIONS	N
10) HAVE COMPLETE CONTROL OVER ALCOHOL	Y		
11) WILL HAVE BETTER APPETITE + EATING HABITS	Y		
12) WON'T GAIN UNWELCOME FAT	Y		
13) " LOSE FITNESS DUE TO ALCOHOL	Y		
14) " " MOTIVATION " "	Y		
15) " " " TO TRAIN	Y		
16) BE ABLE TO DRIVE WHEN I WANT	Y		
17) WILL SET GOOD EXAMPLE TO SONS	Y		
18) IT WON'T CAUSE FAMILY DIVISION	Y		
19) I WILL BE ABLE TO THINK RATIONALLY	Y		
20) MY OVERALL PHYSICAL HEALTH WILL BE BETTER	Y		
21) " " EMOTIONAL " "	Y		
22) WON'T BE EMBARRASSED OR ASHAMED	Y		
23) GREATER INTIMACY WITH DONNA	Y		
24) BETTER RELATIONSHIPS WITH FRIENDS	Y		
25) GREATER RESPECT FROM OTHERS	Y		
26) FAR BETTER SELF-ESTEEM	Y		
27) WILL SAVE LOTS OF MONEY	Y		
28) CAN DO MORE THINGS WITH FAMILY	Y		
29) " " " TO ADVANCE PERSONALLY & IN BUSINESS	Y		
30) BETTER FOCUS EVERY DAY AT WORK	Y		
31) ALWAYS ADHERE TO MY VALUES	Y		
32) I WON'T EVER BE DISAPPOINTED BY MY INTOXICATED BEHAVIOUR	Y		
33) I WON'T BE ONE OF THE ORDINARY CROWD THAT FOLLOWS SUIT	Y		
34) FREE TO FOLLOW MY DREAMS AND FULL POTENTIAL	Y		

Assignment: Element 7

Go to the Element 7 worksheet in your Element Workbook and record your answers to the following:

1. In the "Combined Perceived Benefits of Ceasing Alcohol" column add all the individual advantages and benefits of ceasing alcohol consumption from the assignments for Elements 4, 5, and 6. (This will be done automatically if you have used the Element Workbook spread sheet file available at Alcohemy.com)
2. In the "Combined Perceived Benefits of Alcohol" column add the individual perceived benefits of drinking alcohol from the assignments for Elements 4, 5, and 6. (This will be done automatically if you have used the Element Workbook spread sheet file available at Alcohemy.com)
3. If there are identical reasons in multiple elements, you only need to add it to Element 7's list once to keep it concise.
4. Once you have completed your combined lists, review your current values from Element 3. Then note in the "Aligned to Values?" column next to each combined list whether each item is aligned to a current value of yours or not. You will most likely find that the reasons to cease alcohol all align with a positive healthy value and the reasons for alcohol use don't.
5. Print out your completed sheet to keep your reasons for ceasing alcohol visible to you every day and read them for motivation during the ceasing phase.

ELEMENT 8

RECORD AND REPLACE THE FEARS THAT ARE HOLDING YOU BACK

In Element 8, we examine the fears you have that are based on your old and current beliefs. The belief that you need to consume alcohol to achieve some of the states of mind and accomplishments that you desire elicits fear when you contemplate changing that habit. Seeing the overwhelming evidence that regular alcohol consumption is a destructive habit in your life is one thing; overcoming the fears of changing it is another. Contemplating and confronting your fears is a key element in any change, and certainly this one. Understanding is the remedy for fear. I can't emphasize enough the importance of reading or listening to quality personal development material, especially pertaining to overcoming fear and increasing belief in your innate ability. Understanding the nature of your fear, gaining knowledge about the source, and being prepared helps eliminate it. By noting what fears you have, you can calmly and rationally investigate new ways you can adopt to deal with those individual issues ahead of time instead of in the moment.

If you know at your core that drinking alcohol harms your mind and body, and that it is not the right thing for you to be doing, when these thoughts surface consciously, you immediately contemplate what your life would be like without using alcohol, and the fear response kicks in. We conjure up mental visions and feelings of what we perceive as negative aspects of ceasing alcohol, like alienation and rejection from friends, lack of social confidence, inability to unwind and relax, being seen as different, turning into a grouch—you can add others, I'm sure. We don't really know these things will come to bear, though the fear of the unknown projects the worst-case scenarios into our minds. We tend to base our decisions on these fears rather than what we know to be true and having faith in our own innate abilities.

Fear is not a tangible, physical thing that is outside our control. Fear is always just a state of mind, and it is made up of the thoughts we are currently having and therefore completely within our control. The only thing we have to fear is the emotion of fear itself, as the object of our fear is not actually real, rather something we think might happen in the future. This fear is often based on outdated beliefs and conditioning that we were taught or we adopted many years ago. When people are fearful of doing something, it is not the 'doing' that is the issue; it is the imagined negative consequence if it doesn't go well. We would all love the thrill of doing new things if we knew it would be a successful and happy experience. We just fear confronting the worst result that we imagine may happen. Therefore we wait and attempt new challenging things only when we are more certain that the outcome will be what we desire. Some don't commit to giving challenging things a determined go until someone can virtually guarantee their success. I have heard and seen it written that it is the unknown that we fear most; I disagree with that concept, and believe it is what we replace the unknown with that causes our fear. Most people would gladly attempt challenges if the outcomes were likely to be successful or even unknown, as long as they wouldn't be worse off. The majority, however, tend to paint the picture of the unknown destination with images of the worst-case scenarios they have conjured up in their minds, and therefore don't commit to the challenge. Think of a time when you balked at a challenge you would have loved to be successful in. I bet it wasn't the visions of success that made you reluctant; it was the thoughts and visions of the worst outcome that held you back.

The amount of reward and sense of satisfaction that we get from even attempting a difficult challenge, let alone successfully completing it, is directly proportional to its difficulty and the uncertainty of your success. Significant challenges with highly uncertain outcomes result in the biggest rewards; huge amounts of dopamine and serotonin are released. Accomplishments requiring lesser effort with predicable results deliver lower levels of personal satisfaction. If we knew the definite outcome of everything we attempted, there would be no sense of reward. Everything would be reduced to a mere calculated task with an expected outcome. Words like "satisfaction," "gratification," "ecstatic," "fulfillment," "accomplishment," "achievement," "euphoric," "proud," "exhilaration," and "inspirational" would lose most of their meaning. It is the unknown factor and the possibility that the result could go either way that makes it a *challenge* and generates our sense of euphoria when we are successful. The greater the unknown factor, the greater the effort required; the more you risk yourself, the greater the emotional reward will be at completion. The trick is that instead of focusing on conjured up thoughts and visions of worst-case scenarios, you must fill your mind and beliefs with thoughts, visions, and emotions of what success will be like when you attain it. Do this and your fear of the future outcome will be replaced by expectations of success and eager anticipation.

It is impossible to have the emotion of fear toward something that has already taken place in your past. If some unpleasant event has just happened, we are not *fearful* of it; instead we experience other emotions that are relevant to the past (such as loss, sadness, anger, regret, guilt, disappointment, embarrassment) as we deal with the consequences of what took place. You may let yourself be fearful of the event happening again or leading to other unpleasant actions, though again all these thoughts are about the possibility of something happening in the future and therefore what you fear is not real. It's all a state of mind which you have the ability to control. They are *your* thoughts and only *you* have the ultimate control over what you think. This revelation alone has been the key to unlocking many a person's potential and freeing their minds to do things they once feared.

Most people become creatures of habit and predictability. When they are confronted with moving outside that comfortable familiarity, the uncertainty of how they will experience and react to the unknown produces an emotion corresponding to how they think about it. A few people will see it as an exciting challenge, adventure, or opportunity to advance themselves by experiencing something new. Most, however, when confronted with something new and outside of their comfort zone, conjure up thoughts and visions of the worst-case scenarios. These thoughts will produce the constrictive and limiting emotion of fear. By habitually adopting "be prepared for the worst" thinking, we tend to block out the possibility of it being a rewarding experience. I'm not saying we shouldn't consider all the possibilities of our actions, but if we adopt "be prepared for the best" thinking, our emotional response will be one that allows us to advance with a positive expectation of success. We tend to filter for and attract to us what we think about and expect. If you are focused on negative outcomes, and therefore emotionally charged with anxiety and fear, then that is what the most likely result will be. If you are thinking about positive outcomes and keeping an excited and expectant attitude, then you will more likely attract the circumstances that deliver those positive results. Our minds focus our attention and actions on what our predominant thoughts and feelings believe should be happening, regardless of whether it is good or negative. Our brain tends to filter out what is not expected and highlight what is anticipated. If you are focusing on negative outcomes, real opportunities could be right in front of you and you won't notice them. You will mainly notice the undesirable aspects in your brain's attempt to confirm your thoughts and expectations. Conversely, if you have a high expectation of success, then all sorts of advantages and support will be presented to you, as your mind and the universe conspire to help and ratify your thoughts and expectations of success.

You will see from the fears I listed in this element that this was a significant challenge I had to overcome. Until I worked through this process, I had many doubts and fears concerning my ability to see this through, what my life would be like afterward, and what others would think of me. I had to recognize these one by one, rationally think them through, and find a positive answer to focus on, so I could therefore override the fearful concern. This start-to-finish habit-breaking process I had developed taught me I did have the drive and ability to do it, that my life would be much better afterward, and that it matters more what I think of myself than it does what other people think of me. By writing down the new positive beliefs and expectations to oppose the old fears, I was able to focus on the new beneficial ones. This had a dual effect of reducing the doubt and fear whilst elevating the expectation and courage. I have included my notes to the right.

You cannot be all you can be and achieve your real potential by being attached to how and who you are now and fearful of losing that. This includes the attachment to what you believe are your physical possessions, lifestyle, and status. As the word "attached" implies, people get bound or shackled to certain possessions, attainments, limiting beliefs, and behaviors. Who you are and all you have at this point in time is a result of who you *were* up until this point. Who you become depends on the choices you make today. When it comes to who you are, if you dare to risk a little, you chance to gain a tad. But if you have the courage to put yourself out there and risk a lot, then you stand to reap huge rewards, beyond your present realization. You need to risk letting go of who you are now to be a better you. Risk standing up and doing what you know or suspect is right, truthful, and honest, and life will pay you back in abundance. Risk connecting with new friends and people who will support you. Being bound up for fear of losing what you believe is currently yours will stifle motivation and the desire to do more, be more, and have more. Only by giving up something of a lower nature, even though it may seem a huge sacrifice, do we make room for something of an enormous higher nature to take its place. It is only when we are unafraid of losing what we believe we have that we are truly free to move forward and discover how great we really can be. Be willing to put a face to your real values and desires… your face.

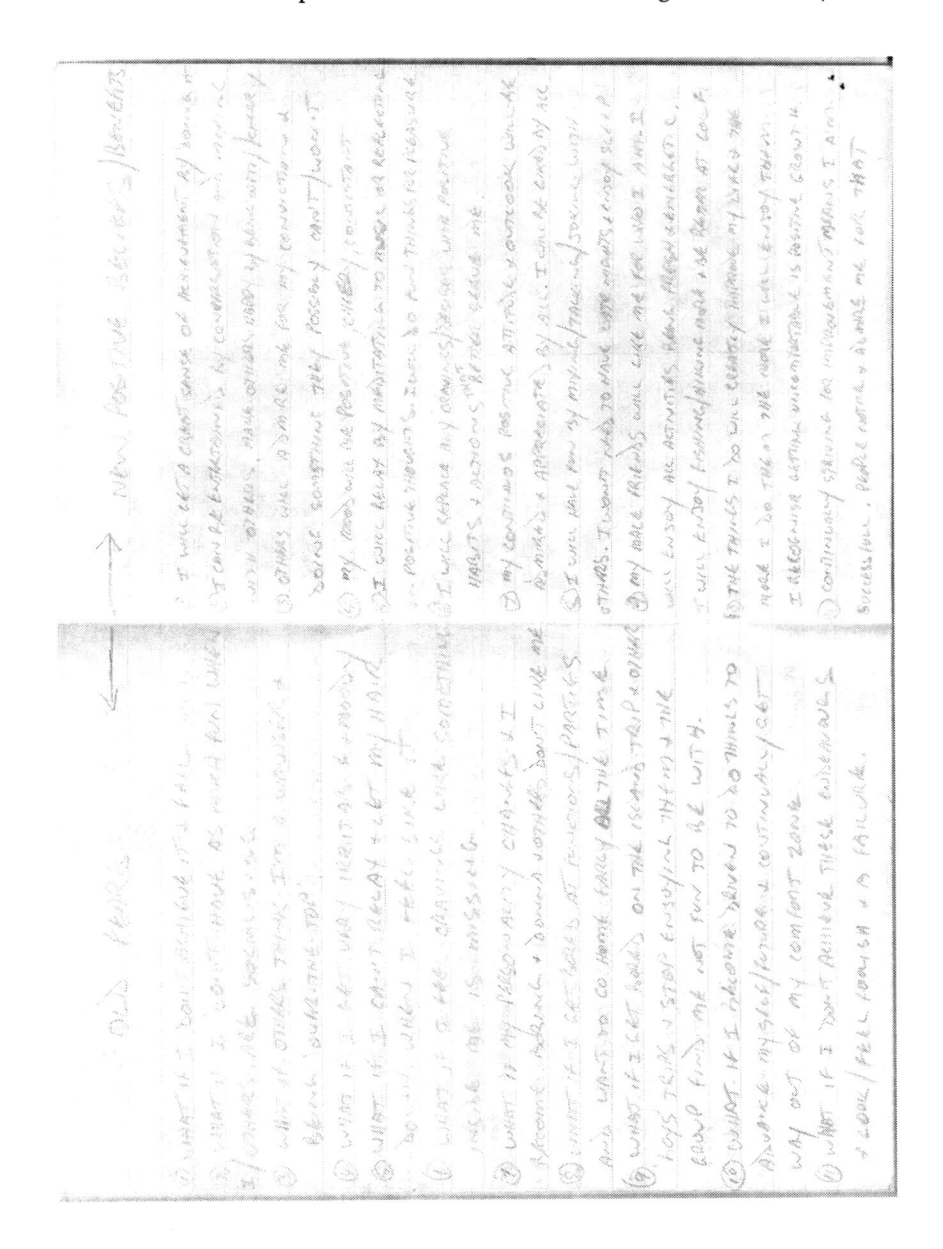

Another fear factor that stifles ambition is the fear of being considered different from current friends and associates. As I'll discuss in more detail in Element 10, people with similar ideals and habits have a tendency to group together so they feel comfortable and protected and have a sense of belonging. This is a good thing if the group has great values and is focused on the positive advancement of the individuals or other worthy causes. However, if the group has formed around a negative ideal or habit, it is a group of individuals you should distance yourself from if you are to follow your own path and develop your unique aspirations. Taking a step like this away from the commonality makes you stand out as different, and you can lose the sense of group comfort, protection, and belonging. The images that we create in our minds of what the negative repercussions may be generate a fear of letting go of the old world. Instead of focusing on the likely positive aspects of being different from those we normally associate with, we tend to fear being labeled as 'different' as we place a negative connotation on being different. Although this is a very real fear for those folks, it is really something that should be welcomed and embraced. Every famous person who has achieved greatness in their life did so because they chose to become different from the crowd. Famous people were mostly ordinary people like you and I who had the courage to choose to be or do something different.

It is bewildering when you really think about it. We are all born as unique individuals (even identical twins have a different spirit and personality), yet most people spend their lives trying to be the same as other people they like or admire, more than themselves. The reality is that you can never be the same as someone else, and it is a shame that people try to do so. Instead, we should cherish and delight in our individuality and strive to be the very best at what our innate desires drive us toward. Conformity to mass thinking and direction is denying your own intrinsic creative ability to construct your life just the way you desire it. Be sure you can place your unique stamp of approval on all things before you accept them. If your inner lifeometer is indicating that something is not helping you on your unique journey, don't be fearful of rejecting it. Embrace the thought of being different from the crowd and draw motivation from the fact that all greatly admired and respected people dared to step outside their comfort zone and become different from the people around them. Not only will being different from people leading ordinary lives deliver you different physical and financial rewards, it will lift your self-respect and psychological approach with everything you do to another level. When you have felt the positive effects of doing it once, it gives you the permission and confidence for it to flow into all areas of your life. Do the things you fear to do and you will become the person you desire to be. The inner power I felt after I had broken through the fear of being different was (and still is) amazing, and I could write a book just on my experience and benefits of that one aspect alone. However, for now, just know that ceasing to conform to the habits and rituals of drinking associates and choosing an alcohol-free lifestyle will make you different for all the right reasons. You will be the one reaping the rewards for the rest of your life.

Assignment: Element 8

Go to the Element 8 worksheet of your Element Workbook and record your answers to the following:

1. Contemplate old and current beliefs then list all the fears you may have about moving to an alcohol-free lifestyle. Include fears about attempting to cease drinking, the process, what happens if you fail, being successful, friends and family, changes to your character, and so on. Add these to the "Current Fears Based on Old Beliefs" column.

2. For each fear you have recorded, write in the corresponding row in the "New Positive Beliefs and Benefits That Replace Them" column a new beneficial and positive way of thinking about the same situation. Record the best-case scenario that would be perfect for you. This is what you will achieve by committing to focus on desires, not fears.

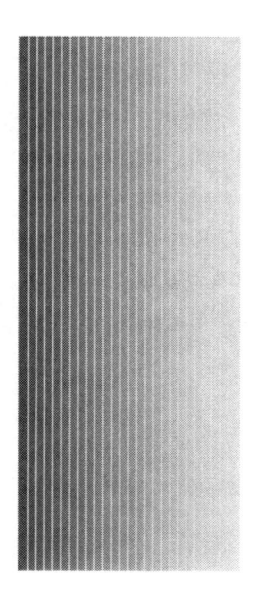

ELEMENT 9

Record Your Current Actions Involving Alcohol and Replace Them with New Actions

This element is a crucially important part of the pre-quitting process. I wanted to be as prepared as possible for as many of the changes that I would encounter in ceasing my alcohol consumption. I knew there would be significant physical and psychological changes required and consequences to these changes. By repetition over many years, my mind and body had been programmed at a subconscious level to act and react in a consistent alcohol-fueled environment. These actions and reactions would continue to occur until by repetition for at least thirty days I forced new and positive habitual actions to gradually replace them. Furthermore, I didn't want to have to try to figure out how to handle these challenges on the spur of the moment when I was perhaps also dealing with cravings to have a drink and not thinking rationally. I wanted to be as clear as possible in my mind how each situation would be dealt with and have a written list to refer to if necessary just prior to those situations occurring.

Record Current Actions and Replace Them with New Actions | 149

ACTIONS TO BE REVIEWED

CURRENT ONES	NEW ONES
(1) Have wine by dinner.	(1) Drink water/apple juice/cordial
(2) " " with dinner	(2) As above, or non-alcoholic wine
(3) Drink extra bourbon watching footy or movies	(3) Any of above (water best)
(4) Have beers at golf club after golf	(4) Drink water or juice (don't stay there long)
(5) " " " soccer club after golf club	(5) Don't stop at club, go straight home.
(6) Having drinks when we go out to dinner every Friday night	(6) Stop going out for a while, drive so can't drink. Drink only water/juice.
(7) Drinking bourbon when playing pokies	(7) Don't play pokies
(8) Having free drinks at Qantas club members lounge	(8) Satisfy cravings with tasty food, drink apple juice, listen to meditation music
(9) Drinking with work colleagues when travelling away with work	(9) Make excuse not to go to bar, or use excuse 'have to work later' not to drink
(10) Going to the casino to drink + gamble when away with work	(10) Make excuse not to go, or use health kick excuse not to have alcohol
(11) Having a few relaxing drinks after a hard gym workout	(11) Have just a filling protein drink to feel satisfied.
(12) Start thinking about having drinks early afternoon on weekends	(12) Plan other fun activities with family, meditate or personal growth activities, creative thinking, be active.
(13) Feeling like having alcohol when I feel hungry	(13) Eat or drink protein-rich healthy foods. Small amounts often.
(14) Feeling like having alcohol when I'm stressed or upset	(14) Use other relaxation techniques, meditate, focus on positive things. Study personal growth material on how to rise above common stress.

Spend some time to reflect on all the occasions when you do (or are tempted to) drink or purchase alcohol. Consider how you can best handle those regular situations to ensure you do not drink or purchase any. It may be that you choose a favorite non-alcoholic drink as a replacement, or temporarily avoid those situations altogether until you are more settled in your new alcohol-free mindset. Contemplate changing your general routine to disrupt your usual alcohol triggers until you are fully in control of saying no to alcohol. Have dinner outside in the pergola/veranda instead of inside or at the usual dining place. If you usually drink while watching TV, do something else instead, like going for a drive or to the cinema. Don't go to the bar to socialize after work for a while, take up a sport or hobby.

Go straight home after sports instead of staying for drinks. Vary the type of food you eat, do things that inhibit and prohibit drinking alcohol, and start or change your exercise routine. Be creative to think of things to do or change that alter your habitual behavior, especially if it is linked to your alcohol consumption.

Understanding Your Alcohol Triggers

Anything you closely link to your habitual alcohol consumption is on its own a potential trigger for your desire to drink. Many additions and dependencies have associated triggers, and they can be different for each individual. Triggers can be things like a smell, type of food, music or sounds, time of day or night, a particular movie or TV program, rainy weather, a place or particular person or group of people. Anything that you closely associate to your habit can be a trigger that may signal to your brain that you should be now engaging in that habitual behavior.

You will need to plan how to deal with these triggers before you begin abstaining from alcohol. Those usual triggers will stimulate chemical and physical reactions in your body that will prime you to be expecting alcohol. This is when you will feel the cravings and possibly withdrawal symptoms the most. If you are a heavy drinker of alcohol, then it is best that you avoid as many of these associated triggers as possible in the early phase of your abstinence. If you follow the pre-cease process I did, your new robust psychological sense, belief, and commitment will have helped diminish or at least override any temporary cravings. However, I strongly suggest that for the first thirty days you avoid as many of your particular alcohol triggers as possible. Having said that, it is not wise to try to change two entrenched habits at the same time. For example, drinking alcohol and smoking cigarettes often go hand in hand. I would not recommend trying to quit smoking and alcohol at the same time. Research has shown that the stress on the mind and body of dealing with two significant changes can derail both endeavors. Staying focused on one at a time will direct your energy to a single goal. I suggest if you have both a smoking and an alcohol habit that you give up alcohol first. I know from personal experience that trying to overcome the cravings associated with nicotine withdrawal when your reasoning and judgment have been affected by even one or two drinks is very difficult. It is usually the case that smokers feel like a cigarette after a drink of alcohol, not crave a drink of alcohol because they have had a cigarette. Anyway, that's another habit I conquered and perhaps a story for another day. I strongly recommend focusing only on the alcohol habit and having a plan developed for all the triggers you can think of that you associate with it. Some triggers you may be able to avoid altogether, while some may be rescheduled to a time of day where drinking alcohol is not an option. Others may be unavoidable, and you may need to review your commitment statement and notes you made during the pre-ceasing review work before being exposed to those trigger situations. Either way you have the absolute power within you to withstand and conquer temptation, and it gets easier each time you do.

Understanding and Avoiding Cravings

Craving for alcohol symptoms is something you may experience in varying degrees and you need to have an action plan for. However I want to stress something very important about cravings that I discovered on my journey. The physical and emotional sensations I felt when I craved something (no matter what it was) were essentially the same. It didn't seem to matter what was triggering the craving, whether it was a craving for food (or a certain type of food), for a drink (or a particular type of drink), for a cigarette, or alcohol. They all seemed to elicit the same basic craving sensation. I would feel like something deep inside me was missing and I had the strong desire to fill that empty and desperately longing void. The sensation didn't appear to be coming from my thoughts or mind, nor from my stomach or other physical part I could pinpoint. It seemed that some intrinsic need at the very core of my being was crying out to be satisfied. The research I have read indicates that cravings are tied into the brain's adaptive release of the reward neurotransmitters glutamate, dopamine, and serotonin. When something we depended on to make us feel good is stopped, we miss these feel-good chemicals and crave the food, drink, substance, or activity that was triggering these chemicals. It is primarily the feeling good or the temporary high we really miss, not the actual external substance. Our brains generally don't care how we get that good feeling (or high), as long as we continue to get it. Therefore, if you were a drug-taking, alcohol-dependent, cigarette-smoking binge eater and one of these reward triggers was not available, you could satisfy your dopamine/serotonin fix by substituting with one or more of the others. Drug rehabilitation centers commonly use methadone as a better replacement for heroin. You may have heard or experienced that when people give up smoking, they tend to eat more food. For some, a lot more food! It also happens that people confuse or deny what it is that they are craving and increase the intake of the wrong trigger substance. A good example is when smokers or alcohol drinkers get hungry and experience a craving for food; they may mistake this craving for the need for a cigarette or drink of alcohol and satisfy it with one of those intakes. People with serious smoking or alcohol habits and a very tight budget can continue to get their brain reward chemical fix by sacrificing food in favor of cigarettes or alcohol, much to the detriment of their health.

One of the main reasons I believe this is *very* important to breaking an alcohol habit is the confusion that can exist as to what is actually causing some of the cravings you will feel while abstaining. I learned during the time I spent giving up the habit of smoking cigarettes that it was very easy to mistake the feeling of hunger for the need for a cigarette. I realized that when I became a bit hungry, I often felt like having a smoke; after the cigarette, the hunger sensation would be relieved. In fact, I could have (and should have) easily satisfied the dopamine/serotonin fix by simply having a small healthy snack. My body and brain were mainly looking for dopamine, and I was choosing the wrong option by having a smoke. A similar thing happened when I was a regular alcohol consumer. I would mistake the desire to fill the need for food with the desire for alcohol, as the craving sensations were similar. If the time of day was acceptable to me to have an alcoholic drink, then that would sometimes take precedence over food. To further confuse the two cravings, regular consumers of alcohol often combine the alcohol with food as standard practice—for example, a few glasses of wine or beer with lunch and dinner, a few glasses of wine, beer, or spirits with snack food or tapas, and so on. This also can lead to them believing it is really alcohol they are craving when in fact they may just be a bit hungry. Psychological triggers also come into play when the two are strongly associated with each other. Sitting down for lunch and dinner can trigger the psychological expectation that alcohol is also required, and this in turn can increase the physiochemical craving for it. In this case if you were to be given a drink that you believed contained alcohol (though it didn't), you would still be satisfied. As stated earlier, research has shown that the belief you are consuming alcohol can elicit the same psychological and physiological responses as actually having alcohol.

The important lesson here is to not assume it is alcohol you are craving. It may just be a lower than expected dopamine level that can be just as easily resolved by having another rewarding experience, like eating something delicious and healthy or some other pleasurable drink or experience. Remember that it is the good feeling (or high) you are desiring, not the actual ethyl alcohol that you have formed a habit of depending on to trigger the feeling. Dopamine is dopamine, and your brain doesn't care how you choose to trigger it, so choose something that supports you, not harms you. I would choose to eat a bit more (and even temporarily put on a little bit of weight) during a period of ceasing alcohol or cigarettes, rather than suffer the long term harm alcohol and smoking will do.

As with all habits our minds become conditioned by repetition to a point where you do things unconsciously. This is a very positive adaptation for most of our everyday habits, and it serves us very well. Imagine if each time we had to give too much thought to brushing our teeth, getting dressed, picking up a glass of water and drinking from it, turning the handle on a door and opening it, walking, typing on a keyboard, and so on. Here's a good one: using your tongue to push food around your mouth and teeth so it gets chewed properly before swallowing. You had to learn how to do that to some degree as a young toddler without biting your tongue, and now you don't even realize you do it until a piece of food gets stuck and you have to think about where your tongue needs to be to move the food. If you actually focus on your tongue while you are chewing normally you will notice your tongue is extremely busy and doesn't stop moving, while it very rarely gets bitten. Imagine if you had to concentrate on doing that all the time. We develop many helpful learned habits when we are very young.

My long-winded but hopefully enlightening point is that if we do things often enough, they become habits. This includes things like snacking on certain foods, drinking tea or coffee, smoking, gesturing with your hands when talking, and, yes, drinking alcohol.

Therefore, consider what you do with your spare time and choose things that benefit you in some way. As stated in Element 8, I suggest you regularly read or listen to positive personal development material that fosters helpful values and renewed belief in your innate abilities. You may have spent years being conditioned to believe your life has been mapped out and you are what you are and there is no changing that. Perhaps you have been battered into submission by circumstances and negative influences, and therefore have decided that settling for what you have and are now is acceptable and it is as good as it will get. It is essential you learn the delusion of that wrongful thinking and begin reconditioning your mind to the reality that you have an intrinsic ability to become, create, and accomplish anything you choose to. If you want real and permanent change, you need to adopt the correct mindset, and reading or listening to these types of positive coaching on how to do so will give you the belief and motivation to break free. I have listed on my www.alcohemy.com website some of the books and programs that got me started down the right path and helped me continue my personal development over the years. I started out reading a lot of personal development books, though now I prefer audiobooks and programs to make good use of the time I spend traveling in a vehicle or on a plane. I have not listened to a commercial radio channel or music CD in my car for years, in favor of audio material that furthers my knowledge or particular goals. If you are serious about making significant positive changes in your life I strongly urge you do the same. To change your results you need to change your actions; to change your actions you need to change your predominant thoughts, feelings, and beliefs; to change your thoughts, feelings, and beliefs you must be regularly exposed to new beneficial information that promotes your personal advancement. In essence you can't be exactly the same person you are right now doing the same things and expect different results. You will also find plenty of helpful information and support at my website, alcohemy.com.

Suggested Food and Beverages to Minimize Cravings

The types of food and drinks you choose can also influence the degree of cravings you may feel, so you will need to consider changing what and when you eat and drink as part of your actions. Regularly consuming drinks and foods high in sugars, caffeine, or carbohydrates can increase or enhance cravings. From my research, I understand it is the drop from the high levels of these ingredients after consuming to low levels that stimulates cravings—the crash after the sugar or carbohydrate high. Even though too low of a blood sugar level can stimulate cravings (including for alcohol), I suggest you don't consume a lot of high-sugar or high-carbohydrate foods. This will only instigate the crash effect. The aim is to get your blood glucose level appropriate for your level of activity and maintain it, not have it spiking up and down.

If you currently have a high-sugar diet, the best way is to slowly get your body used to lower and more even levels. I suggest that several weeks out from your planned alcohol cease date you reduce the amount of high-sugar and high-simple carbohydrate foods and drinks you consume as much as you can. From day 1 of ceasing alcohol, maintain constant lower levels of sugar, complex carbohydrates, and caffeinated food and drinks. Eating as much whole, unprocessed, low-glycemic foods will help with this. These food types will also help with a healthy supply of the B-complex vitamins; vitamins A, C, and E; magnesium; selenium; and zinc—all of which are important for protection and health. A good-quality vitamin supplement may also help optimize your intake. Instead of foods like candy (sucrose), cookies, cakes, and chips, choose complex carbohydrates made of whole grains, wheat, or bran. Whole-grain pasta, brown rice, and oatmeal are energy-supplying carbohydrate food options that also provide vitamins and minerals for healthy nervous-system functioning. Be careful with fruit, as it is usually high in sugar (fructose); choose a fruit that is slow to release energy, like bananas. For all my adult life I had very little desire for soft drinks or sweet foods like candy, chocolate, cakes, cookies, and so on, though I must admit the desire did increase after I stopped drinking alcohol. I still don't eat much of these foods now and usually choose low-fat, low-sugar options if I do. That said, I would much rather you temporarily have a small amount of sweet food to appease a craving than any amount of alcohol.

Both acute and chronic consumption of alcohol interferes with production and hormonal regulation of glucose (the blood sugar that is very important for proper brain function). Even brief periods of very low glucose levels (hypoglycemia) can cause brain damage. With acute alcohol consumption contributing to low blood sugar levels and low blood sugar stimulating cravings (including for alcohol), it can create a tragic cycle.[11]

The decreased blood level of glucose (by acute alcohol consumption or other means) has another negative effect on the brain's function. Experiments in mental discipline have shown that the brain has a limited capacity to maintain concentration, make decisions, keep self-discipline, or prolong willpower. These experiments have shown that these mental activities are very energy hungry and, when sustained for a significant period of time, your ability to do them deteriorates. The results of these experiments also showed a link between low blood glucose levels and the ability to preserve (or restore) this type of brain function. Subjects that that were unable to sustain these activities with any quality were rejuvenated when their blood glucose levels were replenished to normal.[12]

Have you ever been making decisions persistently for hours, then finally can't make one more because you've have had enough? Have you ever been concentrating on work or driving for a long time, then start to make simple mistakes? Have you ever had the kids squabbling or pestering you for hours, then finally give in to their requests? Have you ever been very careful with what you buy during a long shopping day, only to buy things you didn't plan to at the very end? In general, most of our lives are

---

[11] National Institute on Alcohol Abuse and Alcoholism, *Alcohol Alert* no. 26 PH 352, October 1994, http://pubs.niaaa.nih.gov/publications/aa26.htm; Roger (no last name given), "Alcohol—How Food Can Reduce Cravings," Wild Health, http://www.wildhealthfood.com/how-food-can-reduce-alcohol-cravings.

[12] John Tierney, "Do You Suffer From Decision Fatigue?" *New York Times*, August 17, 2011, http://www.nytimes.com/2011/08/21/magazine/do-you-suffer-from-decision-fatigue.html

like that. Unless you are living your dream life with everything you desire, you are constantly using your decision-making processes and willpower to determine the best of making yourself as happy as possible within your current means. This constant effort can be very difficult to sustain hour in and hour out, day in and day out. People mentally wear down, and at times their ability to make good decisions fails. They feel they don't have the mental energy to make one more good decision—or any decision at all. They default to a primal instinct to have what they want with the least possible energy expenditure.

You can imagine the further impact if someone has been draining their store of mental energy by constant analytical work and decision making, then going home or to a bar and drinking alcohol to unwind. Alcohol, a known depressant that affects the ability to think rationally and make good judgments, additionally hinders glucose synthesis. A combination of these cognitive disabling conditions is a recipe for disaster. Making or even contemplating important decisions should not be attempted if you are mentally fatigued and have been consuming alcohol.

When you are endeavoring to change a habit (such as ceasing alcohol), the early days when the initial effort requires sustained concentration, decision-making, and exerted willpower can be very mentally fatiguing. Throw this on top of the physical changes that your body will have to adapt to, and you will need all the healthy energy your body can get. As the experiments I mentioned above revealed, having a steady and appropriate level of glucose in the bloodstream and brain will help you maintain the quality of these functions. Having appropriately sourced nutrition (including glucose) will help prevent poor decisions from mental fatigue and inappropriately taking the easy way out by resorting to your old behaviors.

I know not eating regularly enough was my downfall and a trigger for what I thought was an alcohol craving. I have a fairly fast metabolism from a lifetime of sports activity, including triathlons, marathons, and weight training. I seem to burn up my calorie intake fast, and my blood glucose levels get depleted. When this happens I get a strong sensation of emptiness and needing fuel inside me. If I haven't eaten for a while and my blood sugar drops too low, I even get jittery and irritable.

For most of the years of my alcohol dependency I would confuse this craving with the need for alcohol. The sugars in the alcohol drinks I had would bump up my blood glucose so that the effects of alcohol would give me the perception I was feeling much better. Instead of having a small nutritious snack (what my body really needed), I would drink on an empty stomach. Combined with a brain low on glucose and already fatigued, it was a recipe for disaster, often resulting in very poor decisions.

Even in later years before ceasing alcohol, when I knew it was food my body was really craving, at times I still chose to drink instead of eating and raising my glucose level. I knew if I ate a small healthy protein snack and a glass of water, the craving would subside. However, by then I was well and truly dependent on alcohol to feel good, and this craving I was feeling was my psychological excuse to have a drink or three. My way of thinking was if I ate and felt satisfied, my desire to drink wouldn't be as intense; if I didn't desire to drink, then I would miss out on my known habitual way of feeling good. My dependency on alcohol to feel good was overriding my new awareness that the craving I was feeling was not for alcohol, but something to eat so that my blood glucose could be restored to an appropriate level. This is even more important if you have been doing mentally fatiguing work for sustained periods.

Perhaps this is why I experienced an increase in the desire for sweeter foods when I ceased any alcohol intake. My glucose supply was being depleted by the mental energy and willpower I was dedicating. The secret, though, is not to binge on sugary foods or drinks, as this will create a crash/craving cycle. Rather, adopt a lower yet steady level of blood glucose by regular ingestion of quality nutrition. Even now on some days when I need my full concentration sustained all day, I may add a small quantity of dextrose powder (glucose) to my usual pure water drinks in the afternoon.

As an additional way of reducing cravings, I also suggest you increase the amount of lean protein that you eat and drink. I already was enjoying a high-protein diet from years of exercise training, especially gym work and weight training, so that was not a big adjustment I had to make. I was fully aware from my previous training research that quality protein is not only essential to maintaining healthy muscle mass and body function, it greatly reduces any cravings I have when cutting back on total food intake during my periodic body fat cutting phases. These phases may last four to six weeks, and having regular snacks of quality protein kept cravings for food at bay. These snacks consisted of things like small portions of cooked chicken breast, tuna, lean beef, high-protein/low-carb drinks and bars, unsalted raw mixed nuts, and so on. Regular high protein intake as also been shown help with mood, sleep, and digestion.

You should be now well aware of the function of dopamine (pleasure/reward) and serotonin (mood/well-being) in your body and their effects on your feelings of pleasure and well-being. Your body makes serotonin from the amino acid tryptophan. You can increase levels of tryptophan by eating turkey, walnuts, almonds, pecans, chestnuts, pumpkin seeds, sesame seeds, black-eyed peas, Swiss cheese, gruyere, and cheddar. Other foods that provide lesser amounts of tryptophan are whole grains, dairy products, and rice. Almonds, sesame seeds, pumpkin seeds, and dairy products also help produce dopamine. These foods calm the nerves and help in stress management. Tyrosine is an amino acid that triggers dopamine production and keeps your brain alert. It is found in cashews, pine nuts, pistachios, hazelnuts, Brazil nuts, and whole grains. Tyrosine is also found in yogurt, cheese, milk, cottage cheese, turkey, chicken, soy products, fish, avocados, bananas, peanuts, almonds, pumpkin seeds, sesame seeds, and lima beans, according to the University of Maryland Medical Center.

Notice that many of these foods are also good sources of hunger- and craving-reducing protein and are ideal for snacks. It is handy to have a container of the nuts in this list in a drawer at work or handy while travelling. The more you feel hungry and the lower your blood sugar, dopamine, and serotonin levels, the greater the confusion and temptation there is to opt for the wrong craving solution. The risk for people with alcohol dependency is confusing these natural cravings for the craving for alcohol and assuming that having an alcoholic drink is the only fix. You must adopt natural and healthy ways to feel good and emotionally and physically satisfied. Doing so will alleviate the need for alcohol or drugs.

It is also very important to drink plenty of water as part of your new routine. The water composition of a mature adult body is approximately

60–70 percent, and every function of your body depends on it. It is best to have six to eight glasses of natural water a day. Don't count high-sugar drinks such as soft drinks, as they can actually help dehydrate you. The average person does not drink enough water and is often in a regular state of dehydration. If you are leaving it until you are feeling thirsty and craving a drink of water, then you are already dehydrated. By drinking small amounts of water frequently throughout the day, you will prevent yourself from becoming dehydrated and reduce the craving to drink alcohol. It is easy to confuse one craving with another, so it is important to prevent as many of the natural cravings as possible (e.g., food, water). If you think that you are craving a drink of alcohol, have a large glass of cool natural water and you will be amazed at how the craving will disappear. Combine that with a protein snack and you'll be pleasantly satisfied. I drink a large glass of natural water first thing in the morning (after a naturally slow dehydration during the night's sleep) and then a few mouthfuls approximately every fifteen minutes or so during the day. Good hydration is essential for the healthy function of every body part and system as well as to continually cleanse and detox your body. I would rather have to empty my bladder a once or twice more a day than suffer the consequences of perpetual dehydration, which include premature aging.

Although the diuretic properties of caffeine are less active in habitual coffee and tea drinkers, it is a nervous system and metabolic stimulant and can produce clinically significant physical and mental dependence. Caffeine will produce its own craving response to withdrawal for medium to heavy users, which could be confused with alcohol craving. Therefore I suggest you consider this during the early stages of ceasing alcohol and note it as another substance you may like to stop taking in the future. Don't confuse the craving for tea or coffee as the need to have a drink of alcohol. About the only beverages I drink these days apart from water are the very occasional glass of non-alcoholic red wine (good antioxidants) and an infrequent glass of unsweetened apple juice (good electrolytes and low glycemic index). I am more likely to have these types of beverages when I am at social or formal lunch or dinner, in addition to a glass of water.

Your replacement activities that give your 'feel good' serotonin and dopamine levels a boost (thus keeping you feeling satisfied as much possible) should be many, varied, and not all food related. They can be anything that you feel good about doing and that give you a sense of satisfaction or being happy. It can be as simple as reading a motivational book; watching a great inspiring movie on TV or at the cinema; reading or watching comedy; playing a card, board, electronic, or other form of game; catching up for a chat with good friends; regular acts of kindness to others; or, yes, even having sex will do the trick. So there's a good practical reason (to put to your partners) for you men and women who are feeling the desire to increase the frequency you have sex—a great opportunity to contribute to the team effort!

Make a full list of the things you like to do that make you feel good, happy, and content, perhaps ones you haven't done for some time. Keep in mind your childhood passions. Choose some for different times of the day, different days of the week, and different situations you usually encounter. Things that tend to make you smile a lot or laugh are very good at raising serotonin and dopamine, and they repress any cravings or the sense you need something to feel better. One thing that I used a lot was the very calming and relaxing benefits of meditation. It is a natural way to increase serotonin and dopamine levels, and it has many other health-related benefits, including lowering stress and decreasing blood pressure. Apart from general meditation music, I also got great benefit from using a personalized version of Bill Harris's Holosync meditation technology. I also studied self-hypnosis and used a combination of that and meditation to relax and affirm a positive and successful attitude. Regular massages are similarly a good way to feel great, help detox the body, and promote good health.

Instead of wasting your time drinking, find a purpose that not only serves you, but also will benefit others. Similarly, another truly great way to raise your sensation of gratification and reward is to do kind acts, or give more of yourself to others or worthy causes. Join a cause or create something worthy that is greater than the value or return you think you get from alcohol, something you can do that will generate a great deal of satisfaction and dwarf the sense of well-being you believe you get from drinking alcohol. There is a universal law of energy that proclaims the more you give of yourself, the more you will receive back in return; conversely, if you give little, you will receive little in return. This is true no matter what it is that you give. If you give a lot of love to others, you will receive a lot of it back; give a little, you will only receive a little; give a lot of bad vibes out, receive a lot of bad vibes back; give a lot of your time to others, and others will have a lot of time for you; provide others with a reason to be happy, and you will receive many reasons to be happy; give of your money to worthy causes, and your prosperity will be increased in return. If you don't deliberately practice this energy law to your benefit already, you will be surprised at just how well this law works and just how much satisfaction you will gain when you start to give.

A combination of healthy food and beverage, along with fun and philanthropic activities, usually keeps us feeling satisfied both in the short and long term. There is a great poem by Arthur William Beer (appropriate surname for this book) called "Giving" that sums it up beautifully:

> To get he had tried, yet his store was still meager.
> To a wise man he cried, in a voice keen and eager:
> "Pray tell me how I may successfully live?"
> And the wise man replied, "To get you must give."
>
> As to giving he said, "What have I to give?"
> I've scarce enough bread, and of course one must live;
> But I would partake of Life's bountiful store.
> Came the wise man's response: "Then you must give more."
>
> The lesson he learned; to get was forgotten,
> Toward mankind he turned with a love new begotten.
> As he gave of himself in unselfish living,
> Then joy crowned his days, for he grew rich in giving.

Record Current Actions and Replace Them with New Actions

You will need to carefully consider and plan which of your alcohol and situational replacement strategies is best for you at each stage as you progress. Create a schedule of your activities, foods, and drinks so you aren't acting randomly and therefore more susceptible to impulsive temptations. From day 1 to day 30, avoidance of as many alcohol-related locations and triggers as possible may be appropriate for many, especially if you have not developed a steadfast resolve to see it through by your start date. I do strongly encourage you to work on your determination by reviewing and emotionalizing the results of the internal analysis you have done in the previous elements. The hardest part of this journey is the first few steps you take. Each successive step after that gets easier, and your resolve and confidence get stronger as you stride forward. As you start to experience the positive difference being alcohol-free makes in your life and the confirmation that it really has only an upside, the enhanced belief in yourself will drive you the rest of the way.

Assignment: Element 9

Go to the Element 9 worksheet of your Element Workbook and record your answers to the following:

1. Spend some time listing all of the small actions and habits that you now do that are associated with or trigger the desire for alcohol and record these in the "Current Actions I Need to Change" column. Remember that a lot of these alcohol-related behaviors have been programmed into your subconscious mind and you may not even be consciously aware of some, so you need to spend some quality time thinking about your routines. If you have a friend you trust and can confide in, ask him or her what he or she thinks some of your alcohol habits and triggers are. Include people, places, foods, and situations that will challenge you as you start your alcohol-free journey.

2. List as many countermeasures and replacement actions you can do to support your success and promote your well-being. Until you have rewired your brain and subconscious mind with your

new habitual behaviors, you will have to make a conscious effort to focus on and manage all the small actions that used to make up your alcohol drinking habit. You need constant repetition to make your new list of healthy actions part of your subconscious alcohol-free habitual behavior.

ELEMENT 10

PREPARE ANSWERS TO LIKELY QUESTIONS AND STATEMENTS REGARDING YOUR NEW HABIT

One of the fears I had was how my friends and drinking buddies would react when they found out I was ceasing to drink alcohol. They had to find out sooner or later, so should I tell them up front with some form of statement, or just wait and answer the inevitable questions as they arose? As the statistics I provided in chapter 1 attest, drinking alcohol is an extensively accepted practice worldwide. In countries like Australia, it is generally considered part of our culture to drink socially, and to not do so can be considered antisocial by many. Therefore it is not only close and social friends who would be seeking a reason why I was not drinking, but also work colleagues and other general acquaintances when in situations where alcohol is available.

Certainly at all the social functions and occasions I have attended, the assumption was that everyone would be consuming alcohol except for perhaps those with legal (driving or underage), medical, or religious

Questions + Answers

Possible Questions	Answers
① Why aren't you having a drink?	① - I'm trying to be a bit more healthy - I'm giving my liver a rest - I'm really thirsty & water is the only thing that really quenches my thirst. - I've got some work to do later & want a clear head - I've got to drive (now/later) so rather not drink anything. - Donna usually drives so it's my turn so she can have a few drinks - I've got to be sharp tomorrow for (work/sport/driving etc.) so don't want to drink.
② How long aren't you drinking for?	② - I'll see how it goes. - I don't know, if I like the lifestyle change it maybe forever. - I'll see what my liver and body has to say about it - I'd like to give my body a big break from it so I'll see how it goes - I promised myself I would give alcohol a miss for a few months to really give my body a rest from it. - If I see good results from a short break I make it permanent
③ What made you decide to quit alcohol?	③ - At my age you have to take better care of yourself. - It really was doing me more harm than good. - I want to live the rest of my life as healthy as possible. - I got sick of the feeling that I need to have to drink.

reasons. If I was in a social situation where I was asked by someone going to the bar if I wanted a drink, and my answer was for something non-alcoholic, there would be an expectation on me to also provide a suitable excuse for not ordering something alcoholic: "I'll just have an apple juice as I have to drive" or "I'll just have a water as I have some important work to do straight after." In Australia, especially with people of my generation, the presumption is that everyone of a legal drinking age (and often younger) does drink unless they have a special reason not to. Unfortunately it is considered normal to habitually drink alcohol (particularly to "enhance" social occasions) and widely considered abnormal if you don't.

It is possible you may get negative comments from some friends and associates about your decision to be alcohol-free. Remember that these are only invitations for you to react. You have the power to choose how you will respond, or if you will respond at all. You get to set and keep your boundaries of what you consider acceptable behavior and decline any invitations to react badly. Being prepared for some likely scenarios means you will be able to calmly and rationally respond rather than react on the spur of the moment and perhaps even give in to the temptation to drink rather than dealing with questions.

Certain people (including family, friends, co-workers, and teammates), in addition to being drinking triggers, may also be unsupportive or even a deliberate hindrance to your success. I certainly encountered this in my early days of abstinence. If you are used to drinking with certain individuals or groups of people in a regular social environment, they are going to question why you are not drinking. If these people are also habitual alcohol drinkers with dependencies of their own, generally they will not feel comfortable that one of their drinking buddies wants to break free from their established routine. There are two key reasons they may not want you to stop drinking, though first let me explain a little why people form groups and are protective of them.

People have a natural tendency to want to be liked and to feel like they belong to something meaningful and important or that they can contribute personal value to. We also have a natural tendency to group together for survival reasons, such as maternal, security, and cooperative living activities. This is a tribal instinct that served us well for many thousands of years. Most people feel more isolated, disconnected, and vulnerable when they are predominantly on their own without any support to fall back on. (This is a reason public support groups like Alcoholics Anonymous are important to people who have no appropriate personal support and feel they can't cope on their own.) People tend to gravitate to others and form bonds and groups with those who have similar likes and dislikes, interests, beliefs, appearance, and habits. People who like golf are attracted to golf clubs and bond with other golfers; people who dislike the thought of the public owning guns form anti-gun lobbies; people who are interested in public speaking, food, cars, knitting, various pets, gardening, or collecting seek out and form groups with others that have those same interests. People with different religious beliefs form groups based on the (sometimes subtle) differences in their beliefs. There is a tendency for people of different ethnic origins and skin color to feel more comfortable in groups of similar people, and even people generally considered attractive or unattractive tend to group with similar people. Within these general examples of larger social groups, subgroups are formed based on the habits people have. Smoking, drinking alcohol, taking drugs, compulsive eating, and aggressive or antisocial behavior are a few negative habits that people tend to form alliances and subgroups around. Regardless of the positive or negative intentions or habits of all these types of informal groups, they serve the purpose of uniting their members with a particular commonality, thus allowing them feel supported, secure, and comfortable that they belong. Most often any disunity from within or challenge from without the group that is deemed a threat to the comfort of the members is met with staunch resistance. People generally don't like change and certainly don't like to be made to feel uncomfortable. Therefore anything that threatens the status quo is unacceptable to them. Using safety in numbers, the members of the group unite to subdue any internal disruption or cast out the perpetrator. If the source of the danger is external, then they band together toward a common good and feel even more united and a greater sense of belonging.

If you are in one or more family groups, social groups, or subgroups and regular or heavy alcohol consumption forms an expected part of that group's activity, then you can expect resistance to any change you wish to make. This is regardless of whether the change only involves *your* habit and not the general activities of the group. Depending on the size of the group and your status and significance within the group, you may be subjected to a little or a lot of retaliation, though be assured your actions of change will not go unnoticed. It can be a bit of a catch-22 situation for you.

We seek and cherish the comfort, security, and sense of togetherness that being part of a like group can provide, yet only we alone as individuals can make a choice to improve ourselves and be successful or not. No one can make *your* choice for you. If 999 people in your group of 1,000 choose to take a certain action, your choice still has to be individually yours. Regardless of pressure or goading to conform to mass thinking, only *you* can choose what is right for you and what you will do. No one else can create your future for you; the final decision is *always* yours alone. Most often the people who choose to leave the comfort of the group thinking and dare to be different are the ones who stand out from the crowd and achieve individual success, success that they never could have achieved if they remained with the mass mentality. Even in positive and supporting groups that provide great coaching and mentoring, it is up the individual to choose how successful they will be and if and when it is appropriate for them to move on in a new direction.

Now back to the two key reasons your changing to an alcohol-free lifestyle will make individual members uncomfortable in your group of habitual drinkers. The first reason is that they will see it as a threat to perhaps a very well-established drinking pattern or schedule that they have and wish to keep. Often people with alcohol dependencies will use other drinkers as the excuse to their family or even themselves, that they have to partake in some social drinking as it is expected of them and would be rude not to. If one of their drinking buddies (or excuses) is removed, this threatens the legitimacy of their own routine. This is more noticeable with smaller drinking groups. If your group is just two of you with dependencies who regularly get together for drinks and one wants to stop and the other doesn't, this would be obviously very significant for the one who doesn't. There would clearly be some direct questioning and perhaps intense resistance or even animosity. This may also leave the remaining drinker feeling vulnerable to pressure from their loved ones who want them to resolve their own alcohol dependency issues. If you were a part of a larger regular drinking circle (like a work or sports social group), then even though the other remaining drinkers in that group would take some comfort in there still being many other drinkers who wish to drink with them, you would then be considered different and treated as such. A few rational-thinking individuals may recognize the benefit of what you are doing and give you encouragement, though you should be prepared that those with alcohol dependencies may try to sabotage your endeavors and make you the target of jokes and gossip. Again, this is because it brings to their attention that they also have alcohol issues of their own and they don't want these to be exposed. The fact that one person is prepared to do something about their alcohol dependence shines the spotlight on everyone else in that group, and others with known dependencies may not like that at all.

I believe we all have a basic desire to be liked and considered important by the groups of people we are associated with. I don't think this is a bad thing as long as the respect we have for ourselves and our own values isn't compromised in the process. What we think of ourselves and our continued endeavor to be the best we can be in all aspects of our life should be our primary consideration in decision making, ahead of the opinions of others. Having said that, generally the higher we perceive our status is in a tribe, the more comfortable we are. Unfortunately this can have a negative impact on our desire to continually improve ourselves. The more comfortable we are with our current status in a group, the less motivated we will be to change, even if the change is highly advantageous to us as an individual. This is especially so if the change could disrupt our comfortable status within the group.

Ask yourself if you would be more comfortable as low-status member of a group of very high performers, or a highly valued and respected member of another group despite the group's general mediocre performance. Even though we know we should choose the high-performance group so we can learn and strive to better ourselves, if we are really honest most would be more comfortable being in the lesser group if it meant we fit in well and had a high status. Therefore, to make personal changes that unsettle your comfort and regard within a group is a challenge that some aren't prepared to face, despite other significant personal benefits.

The second reason drinkers in your group will be uncomfortable is that on witnessing your making an effort to break free and take control of your life, they realize you are doing something that they aren't prepared to do.

These people know they have their own habitual problems and would be better served by not regularly drinking alcohol, and they feel uncomfortable when someone they know makes a committed move to improve their life. They like to benchmark their situation and standing in life against people who are equal or worse off than they are, as this makes them feel better about themselves and their status. Their thinking is along the lines of *I'm doing all right at least I'm not as bad as so-and-so* and *I'm no worse than the rest of my mates*. It lessens their standing in the group if someone else rises above them by making some improvement in their life. It makes them feel a bit less important and insecure that they haven't found the courage that you did to give it a go themselves. It is like they are thinking, *How do they have what it takes and I don't*, and they feel they have less initiative, drive, and ability than you do. Rather than benchmarking their performance against a very high standard and being inspired and motivated by a friend's resolve to improve their life, some will wish you hadn't even considered changing.

Most people don't like change unless they can see that the result is significantly better than their current status and that it is easy to obtain. If others in your group are aware they should make changes but are comfortable with their current status and you strive to make a big improvement in your life situation, this makes them feel worse, not better, about themselves. The easiest solution would be to discourage you or influence your progress to a less successful outcome.

It sounds terrible that family, friends, or colleagues could think and act in ways that would inhibit your success, and I hope that you will not experience this. However, it is a real possibility; hence, I would like people to be prepared should it happen. I personally was confronted with comments like, "What are you going all weird or something?" "Are you turning religious?" "Don't be a dickhead" "When are you going to wake up to yourself and have a drink?" There were also probing questions from people who assumed I had done some alcohol-related thing so bad in my marriage that I was forced to swear off alcohol forever. Even though I was adamant that was not the case and I was quitting alcohol because it was simply and unquestionably the best thing for my life in general, there were some who would not accept that reason.

You have to realize that any negative comments, taunts, or aspersions about your motives or ability to succeed are merely invitations for you to react adversely. You have the power to choose how to respond and decline any invitations to react badly. You set your boundaries of what is acceptable behavior from friends and associates, and you have the authority to respond as you see fit or ignore conduct not worthy of a response. Remember, you don't need their or anyone else's approval to make changes to your life; you only need your own. You be the master of your fate and captain of your soul. Your best response is to simply disregard any remarks by others that aren't affirming your goal. You may acknowledge that they are an opinion, but otherwise let it flow past without concern or effect on your commitment to your desired destination.

At this point I would like to use an analogy that illustrates your best response if you do face opposition or resistance to your intention to live an alcohol-free lifestyle. Just like a mighty river with all its power, you have to start your journey with a small beginning. The headwaters of large rivers usually begin with a trickle started by some melting snow or gentle runoff from a mountain or rainforest shower. Although at this beginning stage the trickle of water is committed to a journey that will see it turn into and be a part of something grand, its power now is comparably weak and it follows a winding path of least resistance. This doesn't detract from its intention to keep moving forward on its journey toward the lake or sea. It simply moves around any obstacles or resistance, such as rocks or logs, it encounters without concern. It has no desire to either engage in a battle with them or retreat from their resistance. It merely acknowledges the obstacles are there and merrily moves on past without expending unnecessary energy. This is following the principles of a natural law of non-resistance.[13]

However, as the trickle turns into a torrent and then a larger stream, the water is more focused and has more power. The more power it has, the more direct path it takes to its destination. What appeared to the stream before as large obstacles to flow around now have less resistance than the stream's natural free-flowing power and intention to stay on path. Accordingly, the obstacles are effortlessly moved aside, again without the concern or need for

---

13 Raymond Holliwell, *Working with the Law* (DeVorss and Company, 2005).

struggle. In time what started as a trickle has developed into a mighty river whose journey can move trees, boulders, and carve mountains into canyons to get to its destination.

Similarly, when you start out doing something that involves breaking away from the crowd or changing expected behavior, like ceasing alcohol, your confidence and ability to sway human obstacles will be slight. Your energy should not be wasted by resisting or fighting against them, but rather focused on the destination of your journey. Let any negativity pass behind you as you flow on by. As you progress and your self-assurance grows in strength, the power that you will project will be enough to brush obstacles aside, as any resistance will be no match for your developing control and resolve. What once seemed to be daunting situations or disparaging comments will now be of little concern as you gain momentum toward your destination of an alcohol-free lifestyle. Furthermore, as time passes and your goal of permanent alcohol-free status is clearly in sight, the energy and power of your majestic river will not only be admired by the former naysayers, but it will also serve as an example and inspiration to them.

I recall an experience where this likeness was very obvious to me some years after I ceased my alcohol habit. Donna and I were traveling on the Andean Explorer train from Cusco to Puno over the Andes Mountains in Peru. We briefly stopped to stretch our legs at the La Raya mountain pass, the highest point of the journey, which was just over 4,300 meters (14,100 feet) above sea level. It was explained to us by our guide that this small flat marshy area around us, which was surrounded by snow-capped peaks, was one of the starting points of the great Amazon River. Water trickles out of one end of this small, marshy, sparsely grassed wetland to form the Vilcanota River, which eventually flows into the mighty Amazon. The water that trickles out the other end eventually forms the Ramis River, which flows into the massive Lake Titicaca. I was standing at a shared starting point of two very significant and magnificent river systems, and all there was to see was a small boggy patch of grassland with llamas grazing on it. It occurred to me that just like many changes we make in our lives, at the very start they may appear insignificant and uncertain about which way they could go and how they will end up. But if we focus on our desired destination, just like these two starting points, our results can end up being as grand to us as the Amazon River or Lake Titicaca is to many thousands of people a year who travel to see their greatness.

So with the possibility in mind that you may come across human obstacles, as part of your preparation before ceasing alcohol and before you announce it to family and friends, you need to prepare some statements about what you are planning. Also prepare some answers to possible questions you are likely to be asked by different people. This way you will not be put on the spot and embarrassingly fumbling for answers under social pressure. You will be able to present yourself in a more assertive, controlled, and committed manner and less likely to have others re-query or continue to challenge your decision or reasons. You become the person with the logically and morally correct motives and hold the high ground in any discussion. This confidence will ultimately serve your resolve for success and also your status in existing social groups.

If you find that no matter what you say to some people, you are still meeting with inappropriate resistance and perhaps negative influence, I suggest you do what the small stream does and just flow on past them without concern, without wasting energy or losing focus on your desired destination. This may mean distancing yourself from them as much as possible during the first thirty to ninety days. If after this time they haven't turned their thinking around to be more in harmony with your new lifestyle, then you need to question what value they have in your new life and whether your association with them is now necessary or desirable. People come and go from our sphere of influence throughout our lives. Some may last a lifetime, and some make only a fleeting appearance. Whether we believe they have had a good or bad effect on us, they all ultimately serve our higher good by the lessons we are meant to learn from interacting with them.

From my personal experience I came to realize I had to distance myself from some of the people in my social group, people whose behavior and thinking weren't in harmony with how I wanted to live my life. This wasn't done in a cold, calculating, or disrespectful manner. Rather, as I deeply pondered how I wanted to live my life, the satisfaction I once felt with some of these associations gradually waned. Some ways of thinking and behaviors that once seemed funny or agreeable to me now were not. My level of ambition was higher, my desire to do the best thing possible was greater, my general attitude was better, and certainly my desire to get enjoyment by sitting around getting intoxicated was gone. I just didn't connect with the energy of some of my social friends and felt the time was right to let some of those bonds subtly drift further apart. You will also experience this and will need to really think about what is best for *you*. You must be prepared to let go of some old habitual friends and associations that aren't in keeping with the better you and supporting your new improved lifestyle. Make sure the groups you are in support your continued personal and professional growth and aren't holding you back.

As part of your alcohol-free preparation, give some consideration to how you will deal with the different situations you will expect to encounter as part of your lifestyle. I had no intention of lying to anyone. I wanted to adhere to my already established code of ethics and to be as honest as their need to know and my privacy permitted. I didn't prepare a statement for family and close friends of my intention to stop drinking alcohol, though I did run through several in my mind. Making some verbal declaration seemed too formal and didn't feel right to me. I wanted others to recognize it as a lifestyle change I had desired to do for health, fitness, and personal development reasons.

So instead of making a statement, I simply chose to let people observe the change for themselves and I responded to individual queries as they arose. The amount of detail I responded with was proportionate to the intimacy of my relationship with the person asking. To my immediate family and long-term closest friends I was open with my answers and reasons to the degree that they wished to delve. I had already conducted the deep and meaningful conversations with myself during my analyzing why I needed to stop drinking and accepted the reasons as fact. If you haven't been totally honest with yourself, it will be hard to be honest with those around you who matter most. To my social friends I kept the initial responses short, though I was open to discuss the situation in more detail if they were sincere in wanting to understand more. To work colleagues or general acquaintances, I would answer with just enough to let them know that I was choosing not to drink on that occasion. It was quite enough most times to simply say, "No, I don't feel like anything to drink right now," or even simpler, "No, I'm fine, thanks." If I was responding to people I did not know, I would sometimes simply say I did not drink alcohol and leave it at that. If asked why, I would state health and lifestyle reasons.

Following are some examples of comments I may have used in the very early days of not drinking. If we were at a gathering of social friends I see from time to time and one asked why I wasn't drinking alcohol, I may have humorously responded, "I've decided to give the healthy lifestyle a go for a while and give my liver a rest," or "Donna has been the designated driver for years, so it's my turn tonight," or "I thought I would give this non-alcoholic wine a go and see what it is like to wake up tomorrow completely healthy." For occasions when I saw the same group regularly, like after golf each weekend, I responded honestly, "I now prefer to drink water after golf as it is really the only thing that quenches my thirst," or I used variations of the healthy lifestyle reason. All of these and other reasons I used were limited in explanation yet truthful in nature. Should anyone want to know more, I would elaborate a little bit extra around desiring to lead a healthier life. If quizzed even further by friends with a genuine interest (not those trying to taunt me), I would then divulge my ultimate intention to have this be a permanent change. During the early weeks of stopping a few people showed genuine interest and support in my decision, though some of my regular social drinking friends either were skeptical or attempted some form of discouragement, including subtle mockery. I'm sure you all have some friends and acquaintances who like stirring people up for entertainment. You don't want to play the victim role and let that behavior deter you from your goal. That is why it is important to plan ahead for how you will deal with current alcohol-related situations (as listed in Element 9) and how you choose to respond to initial alcohol-related questions in this element.

Gauge which family members and friends may be supportive and which ones won't by verbal fishing with comments like, "I'm thinking of giving up the booze to be more healthy," or "I'm considering giving alcohol a miss for a few months to give my liver a good break." The ones who don't respond supportively to those types of statements are the ones you should avoid during your early days of ceasing, or at least be better prepared for whatever comments they may have when you commence. Remember to use the non-resistance method discussed earlier, because aggressive reactions by you take your power away and give it to them. Now that I have been successful in permanently stopping my alcohol dependency, everyone in my social circle knows I don't drink and has accepted it as normal. The only queries I receive from friends now concern what it is like not to drink and how I went about achieving it. You will more than likely find that, contrary to your initial fears, your status within your social connections over time, actually goes up quite a bit due to the fact you've shown courage and resolute commitment. Sometimes it takes only one person's courage to break the mold to give other people around them the permission to do the same. Let that person be you.

Assignment: Element 10

Go to the Element 10 worksheet of your Element Workbook and record your answers to the following:

1. Consider all the alcohol-related situations in which family, friends, colleagues, and acquaintances may have a query or question about you not drinking alcohol and list them in the "Situations or Questions I May Need a Response To" column.
2. For each one, choose how you want to respond. Bear in mind that you may answer the same question differently depending on who asks it.
3. Review your answers before you go into situations where these queries are likely, so you are better prepared and more confident with your replies.

ELEMENT 11

WRITE YOUR COMMITMENT STATEMENT

After reviewing all the reasons you are stopping alcohol consumption and confirmed you have made a resolute decision to see it through to the end, you should write out a commitment statement. It can be as long or as short as you like, providing it captures the feeling and energy behind your absolute commitment to continue your efforts until you are free of the desire to drink alcohol again. This is not an 'objective' nor 'statement of intention'. Objectives and intentions are things you set out to achieve and have a desire to do. This commitment is a clear and definite statement that you will do whatever it takes for as long as it takes to become totally alcohol-free. Retreating and failure are not options. As part of your preparation process before starting day 1, you must start developing the feelings and emotions of what it would be like to be living a happy, confident, energetic, and successful alcohol-free lifestyle. The mere fact that you resolve and commit to do a thing will bring about a change in you that attracts the resources and circumstances to assist you.

> **MY COMMITMENT**
>
> I GIVE MY ABSOLUTE COMMITMENT TO BECOMING ALCOHOL-FREE AND LIVING MY LIFE IN KEEPING WITH MY VALUES. I WILL USE MY DESIRE AND BELIEF IN MYSELF TO STEADFASTLY FOLLOW THIS PROCESS AND WHATEVER OTHER ACTION IT TAKES TO BE SUCCESSFUL IN MY QUEST. I WILL NOT BE BOUND BY ALCOHOL'S GRIP ANY MORE AND BE FREED BY MY SUCCESS. I WILL NEVER BE EMBARRASSED OR SHAMED AGAIN BY CONSEQUENCES OF ME DRINKING ALCOHOL. I WILL NOT LET THE OPINIONS OF OTHERS SWAY ME FROM MY OATH TO BE ALCOHOL-FREE AND WILL LIVE MY LIFE ACCORDING TO MY BELIEFS AND VALUES. I WILL ENDEAVOUR TO INSPIRE AND LEAD FAMILY, FRIENDS AND ALL OTHERS BY SETTING A GOOD EXAMPLE AND ENCOURAGEMENT. I WILL FOREVERMORE BE THE MASTER OF MY FATE, THE CAPTAIN OF MY SOUL.

I strongly suggest you use your imagination to fantasize about the new great things you can see yourself doing when you are free from your alcohol dependency and how good it will feel. The more you can generate the deep internal feelings of what it will be like, the more power you will have. Cut out pictures of places, events, and situations you would like to one day see yourself in and put these in places around your home and office where you will see them daily. The more you see them, the more these good thoughts and feelings will be in your mind and core. The more you embrace and internalize your desires, the more you attract the circumstances to make it happen. This may sound a bit airy-fairy to those who haven't experienced the real and proven benefits, though take my word on it—it works.

For those who are motivated to stop embarrassing incidents and behaviors caused by alcohol use, pick the most troubling and common of these and use them in your statement. Vow you will draw on whatever internal power and courage necessary to be free of alcohol and these incidents and behaviors forever. I suggest you also place your commitment statement in a place where you see it each morning and evening. You can also place a small copy in your wallet or purse to review before going into situations that are likely triggers for the desire to drink alcohol. The statement must elicit strong emotions and expectations of success and the benefits of succeeding. In doing so your mind filters your experience to display opportunities to successfully advance, instead of reasons to fail. If your predominant thoughts and feelings are committed to success, you cannot do anything else but succeed.

Assignment: Element 11

Go to the Element 11 worksheet of your Element Workbook and complete the following steps:

1. Take some quiet time to reflect on all the benefits of being alcohol-free and also some of the key negative impacts you will be free from. Your list at Element 7 will help prompt you.
2. Use these motivators in your written commitment to yourself. Vow that your commitment will remain steadfast until your alcohol freedom eliminates the negative aspects and opens the way for your success. Sign it as a legitimate contract with your soul. Feel

the emotions as you write your statement as the energy of these feelings will be experienced again when you read your statement.
3. Place your statement where you will read it every day for the first thirty days. Put a small copy in your wallet or purse for when you are away from home.

ELEMENT 12

DOCUMENT AND REWARD MILESTONES

Now that you have done the hard part of soul searching, analyzing, and planning, you are ready to put it all into action. This may seem illogical to some; however, if you have spent quality time going through all the previous elements in a completely honest way, you really have already overcome the biggest hurdle of the process of being alcohol-free and you haven't even stopped drinking yet. The biggest obstacle to your success is your mind. It is how you view alcohol's relevance to your life and your current beliefs that make it possible for you to live happily without it.

I have proposed that the three key elements to this and any other significant change are:

- Why: the reason and desire to change.
- How: a proven process to follow.
- Belief: the belief that *you* can do it.

Now that you have these in place and are about to start you will need to create some milestones, or targets of significance, so you can plot and monitor your expected progress, and recognize and reward your success.

Back in chapter 3, I described the NASA experiment that shows the human brain's ability to reset itself when a change of conditions (habit) has occurred for thirty consecutive days. This was my first main target. I wanted to get my brain locked in to believing and accepting that 'not drinking alcohol' was the new normal for me. I knew if I got to that thirty-day milestone, I wouldn't have the ongoing struggle that I once believed I would always have to live with if I gave up drinking alcohol. Thirty days was the first big hilltop to be conquered on this new marathon run, and to make it seem more achievable I needed to break it down into smaller steps.

At the very beginning of ceasing regular alcohol consumption it will be a significant physical and psychological change for you each day, so your efforts need to be recognized at proportionally shorter intervals. For someone like me, who drank alcohol every day for many years, each day of that first week that I did not have any alcohol was a significant step—even more so, given that I knew this was not just another one of my temporary measures, but the start of forever. Sure, I had done my psychological preparation and planning, but this forever approach was scary new territory for me, and each day without alcohol had a new and special significance.

I chose to make my initial milestones each day for the first seven days. Though I am primarily a visual learner, I am a fairly internally motivated person, so the reward I gave myself for completing each day successfully was a mental high five and a pat on the back, along with a favorite food treat at night when I previously would have been drinking. Spending a few moments to mentally congratulate yourself for your success is enough to deliver some good-feeling dopamine to the brain. I also knew that I had stopped drinking alcohol temporarily for up to a few weeks a couple of times (as management strategies) over the previous four or five years, so I wanted to be in the best frame of mind for the sustained effort required ahead.

I would encourage others with an entrenched dependency to recognize each initial day with some reward that is the most meaningful to you. Perhaps it is some special food treat or non-alcoholic drink you particularly enjoy though rarely have. It may be enthusiastic recognition from a partner, family member, or support friend. If you don't have the support of someone else, that is okay. Acknowledge your own efforts in some way, as success is dependent on *your* mental attitude and fortitude, not that of others. Reward yourself in proportion to the effort it took to reach each milestone. For some you may choose things like going to the cinema, getting a massage or pampering beauty treatment, buying some new clothes or accessories, going out for dinner or ordering in special food, having a short holiday, buying a new album—anything that doesn't tempt you to drink and that rewards your success.

I want to mention another situation I encountered that you may also be challenged by. Many times my wife Donna had heard my rhetorical speeches on how I will resolve my alcohol problems. She had witnessed my many alcohol consumption management strategies, with each successive one not delivering the complete results we would have liked. So to avoid the potential of further anticipation followed by disappointment on her part, I worked on the development of what would be my Alcohemy process in secret.

After I had formulated and completed all my pre-quitting processes and was ready start day 1 of being alcohol-free, I simply commenced without any fanfare or announcement to her or anyone else. I wanted my results to do the talking. I was confident I had devised the real deal plan this time, since I was thinking very differently before even ceasing. This was not just another management strategy, because I had the belief that I did not require alcohol at all, and the belief that I could break the habit completely. It was obvious to me after a day or two of no alcohol intake that this was indeed different. I was feeling and thinking about it in positive and permanent terms. Each day and mini milestone that went by I knew I was getting closer to my thirty-day habit-changing brain reset. I was excited and feeling a great sense of accomplishment with each day, then each week, completed.

Even though it would have been very obvious to Donna that I was not having my nightly glasses of wine and weekend alcohol, she had not made any comment at all on my abstaining. I decided to not mention anything to her to see how long it would take for her to say something. I continued to mentally celebrate weekly and then monthly milestones by myself as they came and went. On one hand, I was jubilant that I had passed my thirty-day brain reset milestone and was eagerly looking forward to my back-to-back sixty- and ninety-day milestones. On the other hand, I was disappointed that Donna still had not made any comment whatsoever to me. I was hoping that by this stage she could see that this was different from my management approaches up until that point and would be offering comments of admiration and support, given the significant difference it was going to make to both our lives.

I can't recall exactly how long it took before I couldn't bear it any longer and raised the subject with her. I believe it was around the two-month mark, when we were having a heart-to-heart chat during our regular hour-long, early Sunday morning exercise walk. I said I could not believe she had not made any comment whatsoever about me not drinking, given that this was the one thing she desired most and had been hoping I would do. I said I felt disappointed and hurt that I had finally made a huge breakthrough in being free of my alcohol dependency forever and she had not bothered to make one comment of acknowledgment or support. Donna said she was aware of what I had achieved so far and even though she should have made congratulatory comments, she could not explain why she had not, and she was very sorry for not having done so. After more discussion during that long walk I deduced that the primary reason was that she had been so disappointed by many failed attempts before, therefore she didn't want to get her hopes up again and so dismissed it as another experiment mostly likely to fail.

The point of recounting my experience is if friends and family have seen years dotted with poor behavior and failed attempts at a resolution, their support may not be as forthcoming as you may hope for. Hopefully they will see any serious attempt at resolving your problem worthy of their support and encouragement, though you should be prepared to go it alone if you have to. As I stated earlier, due to pride, ego and public embarrassment I was adamant that I would not go to a support group like Alcoholics Anonymous. However, if you aren't getting the recognition and support you would like from your friends and family around you, and you don't feel like you can cope on your own without some acknowledgment and support, an external support group or professional help may be appropriate for you. As part of my program you will also have access to discreet and anonymous support from me and my international Alcohemy community through my alcohemy.com website. Celebrating your early wins and milestones is important, and although I did this on my own and was committed enough to be okay with that, having some extra support, encouragement, and recognition is a huge benefit.

Depending on your personal circumstances, after you have successfully completed the first week you may choose to follow what I did and set weekly milestones. The first few days of ceasing will be the hardest, though the novelty of it may help get you through it. However, if you have done your homework and preparation as I have laid out in the previous elements, your new way of thinking about alcohol and the effect it has on your life will be the driving force that pushes you onward to success. Weekends are the most likely be the toughest days of the week to maintain your resolve, as these are the days most people socialize and consume more alcohol. Once you have successfully completed your first week (including the weekend),

No Alcohol

30 DAYS

you could plan to move your next milestones to weekly. If you have a particularly substantial drinking habit, you may choose to leave your mini targets daily for the initial two weeks, plus confirm your progress by a daily success acknowledgement and reward. I believe that generally once you have successfully completed the first week or two, weekly milestone targets should be short enough to maintain your belief in achieving the next goal and the required focus to do so.

The thirty-day brain reset was my first key objective as I started my journey. I knew when I got to that target I would be at the top of the first big, steep hill. From there I would be able to see much further ahead and it would be a gradual downhill slope making my journey easier and even more possible to complete. To help reinforce the importance of this, I printed out a big graphic of a bull's-eye target (see above) with an arrow in the center and "30 days" printed along the arrow. I marked off every day until the thirty-day target was met. I understood that it takes a full thirty consecutive days of doing something in a frequent and repetitive manner (or, conversely, not doing something you used to do) to create or break a habit. Not only does this psychologically rewire the brain; research shows that we develop a cellular and muscle memory for things we do repetitively. Just like people who do certain split-second actions repetitively to be become world-class at it (e.g., musicians, cricket slips fielders and wicketkeepers, hockey and soccer goalkeepers, or table tennis players), we mere mortals must also persistently practice good actions to make these mental and physical habits without conscious thinking. Accordingly after this initial thirty days of good actions, my belief and resolve were confirmed and strengthened, and meeting that milestone resulted in even more joy and elation in that my dream of becoming alcohol-free was becoming a reality. The focus and effort I put into preparing and then implementing my plan was paying dividends a hundredfold.

My next goal was to have three, thirty-day milestones accomplished back to back, to take me to the three-month mark. I had already conditioned my body and reset my brain to be habitually free of alcohol. I now needed to cement this as a new way of life. It was now a fact that I could live without alcohol for one month (and without pulling my hair out or going crazy, I might add). I simply needed to repeat what I had done for the first month for another month, and then follow that with one more month. In fact, after psyching myself up and following my prepared plan for the first thirty days, I was surprised how much easier it was than I had once thought it would be. The key was understanding what I had been previously doing and why, understanding why I wanted to change, being aware of what I would be facing and being prepared for it, and having the belief that I could do it. Having done my homework and attained those key elements, I could focus purely on following my plan one step at a time and let the belief and reward keep increasing as a result. An ad hoc, psychologically unprepared approach that is full of doubt and fear, like I had tried in the past, is doomed to fail. Regaining control of your life is far too important to keep taking sporadic potshots at it and having the failed attempts reinforce your belief that you can't do it.

After checking off the second month that passed, and then the third month, my belief in myself and my sense of self-achievement were astounding and powerful. I was now doing something I had once thought was utterly impossible. I obviously don't know what your personal circumstances are or what you have achieved in your life, but I guarantee the sense of power and pride you will feel when you realize you have overcome your dependency will be nothing short of fantastic. What you originally thought of as hard mental preparation work will seem insignificant compared to the physical and emotional rewards you will reap at the end. And this can be achieved simply by diligently preparing and sticking to a proven plan, then checking off the milestones as you achieve them.

After the three-month milestone I knew I was completely in control, though it was important for me to set future targets so I knew my work and focus were not done. Without targets or goals in our lives, we tend to wander aimlessly and risk ending up at a place where we don't really want to be. Having a purpose, plan, and targets keeps us focused on why we are doing something and what we want to accomplish and by when. A ship in the ocean of life with no destination, no map, and no rudder will be controlled by the external winds and current and eventually drift upon a rocky shore or reef to be wrecked. My piloted ship's next port, where I would take on a new supply of reward, would be the six-month milestone. After that it was doubled to a twelve-month milestone, and then yearly after that. Actually, after the six-month milestone I stopped counting the months as they went past and just remembered my original start date as a reference point. Because we tend to think linearly in years, this made the twelve-month milestone a significant timeline event. However, once I had successfully passed the three- then six-month milestones, psychologically I had accepted that I had broken my habit for good and would not be dependent on alcohol ever again.

Regardless of when you are able to genuinely acknowledge that you have no desire to consume alcohol and have broken your habit, I strongly suggest you maintain your milestone recognition and reward system up to at least the twelve-month event, because you will need to remain focused and vigilant for people and occasions that may not present themselves regularly but will test your resolve and response. At twelve months you are still relatively new to saying no to alcohol at formal and social occasions and to people you may find influential or intimidating. You will still come across situations that test your confidence and power to refuse the offer of alcohol and your ability to come up with impromptu reason to explain why you are not drinking. As suggested back in Element 10, you should have rehearsed a number of responses for different situation so you can maintain your confidence and poise. This leaves you and others in no doubt that you are in control of the situation and the decisions and choices you make. It is a good idea to reward yourself (if only with a mental pat on the back) each time you encounter and handle a testing moment, even after the one-year milestone. I still mentally note the anniversary of my start month each year and take joyous pride in stating my alcohol-free status when asked, even now after nearly five years. Any positive reinforcement of your newfound control cements your new way of life in place. Don't be shy in confiding in or sharing your achievements with loved ones or friends who are supporting you. If they are worthy of your friendship they should be very happy for your successes and keen to acknowledge them.

As important as specific milestones are for reward and motivation, I believe that successfully becoming alcohol-free isn't simply measured by the number of days of abstinence. One of the reasons I developed my Alcohemy process the way I did was that I didn't want my alcohol-free status to be rated by numbers (i.e., my success wouldn't be determined by how many days I could remain alcohol-free). The success of my process would be determined by whether I *desired* to have alcohol for any reason. I was successful and free from alcohol as soon as I did not desire to use alcohol for any psychological or physical reason. Depending on the degree of psychological transformation achieved early in the Alcohemy process, this absence of *desire* for alcohol could happen for some people before day 1, others on day 30, and still others three months later. The Alcohemy process is about empowering yourself to be the master of your fate and the captain of your soul—to realize you hold all the cards and can play them however you like. It's all about making choices and taking responsibility for the consequences.

I wish to add a valuable piece of advice at this stage. Life tends to place some of our most challenging obstacles in our way when we are nearing the end of an important journey, as if to ask, have you really learned all the lessons along the way necessary to earn the reward just around the corner? Don't view these challenges as another arduous barrier blocking your chance of success, but rather as a sign that you are very close to the reward you desire. Use the knowledge you have learned (especially the law of non-resistance) and the skills you have developed to stay focused and committed to what will be your greatest assured victory. Each challenge asks a question of you: Are you willing to become *who* you must be to succeed? You give your answer by your results. Those who succeeded in the challenge have answered yes. Those that failed to complete the challenge answered no, whether they knew it or not.

Many a good athlete has mentally given up with only one more bend to round, hurdle to jump, hole to play, lap to swim, or minute on the clock, when victory may have been possible had a renewed and concerted effort been applied when the question was asked. Many a good business proposition or idea has been abandoned because a challenge seemed too hard, just before success would have been achieved after one more endeavor. Great successes demand great challenges, and great challenges demand great courage. The reality is that success always comes after completing the *last* challenge. Be courageous in the face of all your challenges and your success is guaranteed.

Assignment: Element 12

Go to the Element 12 worksheet of your Element Workbook and complete the following steps:

1. Consider how serious your alcohol habit is and how much of an effort it will be to not have any alcohol.
2. Use the milestone frequencies I have suggested in my table or create ones to suit your particular circumstances.
3. Think about what rewards you would like to give yourself at the completion of each milestone and add these to the "My Reward" column.
4. After you have completed Element 13 you can fill in the actual milestone dates in the "Date" column. Day 1 will be the same date as your nominated start date.
5. On successfully reaching each milestone you have set, check it off on the table in the "Reached?" column and record if you took your reward in the "Taken?'" column.

ELEMENT 13

PLAN YOUR START DATE AND *START*

The last element of the cessation process is to plan an appropriate date for day 1 of no alcohol. You should not start the official day 1 until you have fully completed all of the thirteen elements of this framework. It is unwise to take a half-hearted attempt test run to "see how it goes" without fully completing all these processes and fully committing yourself to success. If you are serious about changing your life for the better, no matter whether you consider your alcohol habit minor or out of control, these thirteen elements combine to deliver a comprehensive and lasting solution. If you miss key psychological or planning elements or exercises, you risk falling back into your old habitual ways and damaging your belief that it can be a permanent, life-lasting change.

Cutting back on your usual alcohol intake and making changes to your consumption routine that result in a reduction in overall intake or the times and places you drink is desirable, however. This is psychologically and physiologically different from attempting to cease alcohol altogether. Reducing alcohol consumption during the week or on weekends for several weeks (or, even better, a month) leading up to your day 1 gives your body and brain an advance chance to start adapting to the chemical changes from reduced ethanol in your blood stream. You will not be as dependent on the effect that alcohol has on dopamine, serotonin, and GABA neurotransmitters. You haven't made the big leap into being alcohol-free forever yet, so this isn't as scary as going cold turkey. Also, physiologically, you are only reducing the alcohol-induced reward chemicals, not dropping them suddenly from their usual medium to high levels down to zero. This not only gets you used to the feeling of reduced levels so you are more able to cope; it also allows your body to start readjusting its own biochemical production ahead of day 1.

Element 13 – Plan Start Date

FESTIVITIES I HAVE TAKEN INTO ACCOUNT	START DATE
Rick's birthday 21/Mar	
Anniversary 3/May	26-Mar
No other expected celebrations for 2 months.	

If you wait for the ultimate perfect time to start day 1, you will never commence, though I do suggest you take into consideration important events on your social calendar that would usually involve alcohol consumption (e.g., birthdays, Christmas or other religious celebrations, New Year's Eve, public holidays, weddings, etc.). Try to pick a date in the near future that has at least thirty days before the next significant event. If not, pick a date soon after an alcohol-consuming event to give you as much time as possible before the next one. An even better option is to decline attending functions and events where the expectation to consume alcohol is high until you are past the thirty-, sixty-, or ninety-day milestone, depending how confident you feel about abstaining. Of course, this doesn't avoid the routine and habitual times you may consume alcohol, like perhaps after work, at dinner, while watching TV, after sports, and general socializing. Review the action plan you developed in Element 9 to deal with these day-to-day routine triggers.

I suggest that you schedule day 1 for soon after you have done all the preparation and planning so you are mentally prepared and motivated to see it through to success. Ideally, though, it is best that you have also given yourself a few weeks to practice some alcohol reduction and to test some of your behavioral changes from the action plan in Element 9. Your decision to cease drinking alcohol is the real deal and a life commitment you are making. Therefore, be meticulous in your preparation, choose a start date, and commit to it. Don't procrastinate. Your quality of life is at stake, so don't tinker around with it; be fair dinkum.

Once you have chosen and committed to your start date, whether you choose to announce this publicly to your family, friends, and colleagues is up to you. I chose not to make any formal announcement for my own personal reasons. Announcing and not announcing both have advantages. Which method you decide is best for you will depend on factors like your personality type, confidence level, social and family standing, how obvious it will be to others from the very start that you aren't drinking, and your preference of what motivates you. Making your intentions known to others up front adds weight to your commitment, while it also shows that you have taken responsibility and ownership of the problem and the solution. Also it gives you public accountability for seeing that you follow your plan through to success. Furthermore, other supporters will be aware of your pending challenge, and this gives them the opportunity to make allowances for your change of habit and to provide encouragement and support.

On the other hand, choosing to not announce your intention and start date to your wider group of family, friends, and colleagues can reduce the stress you may feel. The added stress of public scrutiny and monitoring, on top of the initial mental and physical stresses of the alcohol withdrawal process, could be too much for some people. With some people it can be a highly motivating factor, while with others it could feel too intrusive and have a negative impact. Many internally motivated people prefer to work through problems and solutions quietly on their own, while more externally motivated people love the sense of collaboration and community effort.

Another reason for not announcing your commitment to stop consuming alcohol may be that family and friends you commonly interact or socialize with have regular drinking habits themselves and would not support your choice. Even if some of their habits aren't at a particularly harmful level, they may not like others making drastic improvements to their lives. This can highlight their lack of advancement, thus making them feel uncomfortable. These people can deliberately or thoughtlessly sabotage your motivation, confidence, and efforts to succeed by ridicule, discouraging comments, or contributing to temptation. Should your family and friends fall into this category, then you may choose not to initially announce your intentions to them. Instead, you may choose to initially use your prepared statements in Element 10 to allay their curiosity or concern. Only after you have progressed far enough through the ceasing process that you are confident any negativity won't detrimentally affect you will you reveal to them your resolve to permanently abstain.

I'm not promoting dishonesty; ideally you will have family, friends, and colleagues you can openly share your commitment with. But your reality may be quite the opposite, and in those circumstances a little pre-planned creative avoidance may be more appropriate than jeopardizing your success. This is a major change and advancement in the quality of your life at stake here. I think this tactic is acceptable for achieving an outcome in which you and everyone you come into contact with will ultimately be better for your success. It is not as if it will be some long-term, deep, dark secret. It will be a relatively short time before you will be feeling confident, excited, and proud enough of your success to tell people you don't drink. It is simply a suitable means to superb end.

The key is being as prepared as possible before you start day 1. You will know if you have prepared well if you have all your notes from the thirteen elements to refer to and a good sense of purpose, commitment, and belief. Depending on the degree of your alcohol habit, your belief may still be a bit shaky before you actually start, though this is normal and more likely it is nervous tension you are feeling. Don't confuse the feeling of being very nervous with not being ready to start. Most people feel nervous before beginning anything new, let alone a life-changing process. Focus on how great your life will be when you are successful and turn that nervous energy into positive anticipation and excitement.

Assignment: Element 13

Go to the Element 13 worksheet of your Element Workbook and complete the following steps:

1. Consider the formal and social functions and occasions coming up that usually involve the expectation of consuming alcohol. List these events and their dates in the "Festivities I Have Taken into Account" column.
2. Make sure you have completed all the element processes and are committed to seeing your alcohol-free journey through to a successful and rewarding completion.
3. Select a start date that allows you the minimum number of must-attend functions that would usually involve you consuming alcohol over the next thirty to ninety days. Allow yourself a week or two of cutting back on alcohol before the official start date.
4. Put the chosen date in the "Start Date" column.
5. Start on the chosen start date with an expectation of success and reaping the rewards, including tremendous self-respect and the admiration of all around you (whether they admit it or not).
6. Your future has always been in your hands. Reclaim your control by being the master of your fate and the captain of your soul.

CONCLUSION

The Power of Alcohemy

My life so far truly feels like it's been a journey that has taken me full circle: from the mixed feelings of my childhood, which fluctuated from wide-eyed innocence and wonder, to desperate unhappiness and longing to feel joy. From youthful daydreams of adventure and discovery, to my teenage and adult descent into alcohol dependency, resulting in years of despair, frustration, and lost opportunities. It was an arduous journey of more than forty years, but I could never have completed the circle and freed my youthful soul until I finally unshackled the bonds of my alcohol habit, which for so long I believed was helping me.

When I was young and living on our cattle property, life was simple and uncomplicated. Sure, everyone had to work very hard, and we kids were no exception; that's life on the land. Despite the physical and emotional hardships we endured, I also treasure a few great memories and feelings from those early years, but not in the sense of close, loving family, as I don't believe I really felt that. It was more a sense of belonging to something and somewhere, regardless of how tough I felt it was. I was part of this family and part of this rugged isolated land on our property. I felt it belonged to me and I belonged to it. It was a cohabitation that went beyond title deeds or physical location; it was like a merging of identities and souls.

By working the land I had been a part of creating how it looked physically, and the work I put into it helped form my physical appearance and became a part of my psyche. It was my home, and I was mostly free to be completely me. That was the me who loved to ride and trek the hills, valleys, dense scrub, and open grazing land. The me who would think great thoughts and imagine great adventures of travel and discovery. I was creative with my hands and even more creative with my mind and imagination. I was going to conquer the world. Even now it fills my heart with joy just thinking about those free-spirited occasions roaming the hills on my own back then.

However, as we grow older, life presents us with all sorts of unfamiliar challenges. Our youthful spirit of wonder and exuberance often gets lost. If we haven't been blessed with enlightened mentors to guide us through these unchartered waters of growing up, we can be unprepared and risk being caught in a whirlpool that pulls us down or be shipwrecked altogether on rocks. I charted the quickest course to a port that would make me feel better, and I was gradually drawn down into the alcohol whirlpool as a perceived solution. All of my relationships suffered, my athletic potential and aspirations suffered, my academic endeavors suffered, my income-earning potential suffered, and, most important of all, my psyche, imagination, and creativity that were strong and healthy when I was young all withered and barely survived under the shadow of the ever growing alcohol habit weed.

Now after many years of alcohol dependency causing suppressed emotions and persistently feeling stress, despair, embarrassment, shame, humiliation, guilt, a lack of control, and immense frustration of not knowing how to completely escape from it, I have turned a full circle and been reunited with the original me. My Alcohemy process has transformed my life to one of awesome delight, a sense of success, high self-esteem and confidence, regained self-respect and respect for others, and an internal peace and harmony that I yearned for many years but doubted I would ever find. I went from *totally* disbelieving that I would ever be free of my alcohol habit and that I would have to manage it the best I could and bear the negative consequences to now knowing that I have no desire whatsoever to consume alcohol, having no cravings at all, and having no inclination to use any substances to gain pleasure or deal with challenges in life. Before I used to worry every single day about what embarrassing thing might happen if I drank too much, and I was continually on guard. The sense of freedom I experienced going from having a dependency habit to an alcohol-free lifestyle was truly like being released from years of inner imprisonment, bondage, and torture. It was like a dark curse had been lifted or an evil spell had been broken, and I was now free to once again be my real self.

One of the great benefits of successfully completing this alcohol-free transformation, apart from wonderful health and social improvements, is that you become a far better person because of it. The essential inner change you go through as part of the process leaves you with new or enhanced personal qualities that you will benefit from for the rest of your life. I am no longer defined by other peoples' opinions of me; it is my opinion of myself that defines me, and that assessment is completely under my control. This sense of self-control, proven accomplishment, and self-confidence are just a few qualities you will gain. Most important, you get to know the real you a whole lot better. Not the you who for years you have just settled for. Not the you who other people think you should be. Not the you who previously had no belief and confidence to make significant positive changes to your life. You can't embrace the real you when you are regularly drinking alcohol to become someone that is not the natural you; you're only faking it. Therefore you will never be all you can be and achieve the great things that you could by pretending to be who you are not. You will never fulfill your potential while you have an alcohol habit. By being alcohol-free you will know the real you who has the spirit and courage to do what is necessary to achieve what you really desire. You will experience a new side to yourself, one that can draw on the power within you to meet and surmount any challenges of your choosing or that come your way. You will transcend your previous mediocre and complacent expectations of yourself and the life you live and move to desiring more from life and believing that you should and can attain it. You will see the world differently . . . and it will see you differently.

The process of writing down this Alcohemy process for others has shown me how much I have changed in another way. As I considered what to share with others who are struggling with an alcohol dependency, while being as completely transparent and authentic as possible, I felt a need to share some of my deepest, darkest secrets that had remained locked in the vault of my mind for more than twenty years: the infidelities I detailed in chapter 2. I hadn't yet told my own wife and now young adult sons, though I was feeling compelled to share it quite publicly in a book. Obviously I needed to tell them first.

The real power of Alcohemy was revealed when I realized that I was truly a changed man with changed relationships. I finally felt strong enough to share this with Donna and my sons, because I knew I was strong enough on the inside to completely reveal who I was and what I had done, terrible as it was. Though I still deeply regret my wrongdoing, I had faced and defeated the demons that had haunted me for many years, and I was prepared to face whatever challenges we as a family may encounter as a result of the truth. But that didn't mean I wasn't aware that there would be a lot of emotional distress for both Donna and me when I told her. I was also hoping my now adult sons would see it as an alcohol-related human failing and not abandon me when I told them privately after Donna and I had discussed it.

When I told Donna, she was obviously shocked and upset that I had betrayed her trust. Thankfully, though, and as a testament to the type of person she is, after weeks of contemplation she revealed to me she could understand what state I was in back then, though it is who I am now that was more important. Upon weighing it all, she said that she loves the real me now more than ever, and our relationship is now the best it has ever been.

Telling my boys about my serious failings was very difficult. To capture the extreme gravity of the occasion and to use my own heartache in having to tell them as a lesson for other drinkers, I asked my sons if I could record what I told them to clearly show others the real-life repercussions of alcohol abuse, in a hope it may shock others into reconsidering the dangers of their alcohol habit. Again, I was blessed that my sons chose to see it as a serious human failing caused by excessive alcohol and are proud I am using my experience to help others. The actual recording of my revelation to them is available on my Alcohemy.com website, in a hope it helps other parents cease their harmful alcohol habits.

I have absolutely no doubt in the world that anyone, no matter how serious their alcohol habit is, can successfully cease it and live happily alcohol-free by wholeheartedly wanting to and then choosing to do so, drawing on his or her inner power and following the process in this book. If I can do it, anyone can. You just have to give yourself permission. Permission to think great thoughts and imagine the great things that could be possible for you being alcohol-free. Permission to believe that you have as much power and potential in you as anyone else on this planet to follow this plan step by step to a successful and fantastic result. Permission to be different and to break away from people who may be holding you back on your true life's journey.

Just like adventurers and explorers of old had to overcome the fear of risking life and limb to seek out and discover unknown lands, so must we show courage to risk our emotional comfort to discover what our hidden potential is really capable of. It is the greatest journey of discovery you can ever go on. Furthermore, it has the greatest treasures hidden along the way waiting to be discovered. No one else but you can make your journey nor knows the way to your treasures. I don't know what your journey has been like so far, whether your road has been fairly smooth or you have taken the winding, rough, and perilous back tracks. However, I do know that whatever you have to risk of yourself and how much courage you have to draw on, your journey of discovery to find the real alcohol-free you is definitely worth risking your old alcohol-dependent life for.

While you are alive on this planet you owe it to yourself, your family, your friends, and humanity to be the very best you can be. Most of all you owe it to your own creative spirit. Raise the bar by setting new standards for yourself that won't be compromised by negative influences. Instead of following a cultural or group mentality that will never allow you to live up to your full potential, use the Alcohemy process to be alcohol-free and to finally live real, live whole.

It's time for *YOU* to be the master of your fate and the captain of your soul.

APPENDIX:

THE ELEMENT WORKBOOK

Element 1: Your Journey's History

Notes on Key Positive and Negative Aspects of Your Life Before and After Starting Alcohol

Element 2: Record Your Associations with Alcohol

Event/Occasion	Belief/Lesson	Positive Impression?	Conflict with Values?

Element 3: Record Your Life Values

What Values Did I Learn Back Then?	From Where or from Whom Did I Get Them?	Are They Still Valid Now?	If No, What Value Has Replaced It?

Element 4: Record What Alcohol Does for You

Perceived Benefits of Alcohol	Perceived Negative Impacts of Alcohol

Element 5: Record the Effects of Ceasing Your Habit

Perceived Benefits of Ceasing Alcohol	Perceived Negatives of Ceasing Alcohol

Element 6: Record the Effects of *Not* Ceasing Your Habit

Perceived Benefits of *Not* Ceasing Alcohol	Perceived Negatives of *Not* Ceasing Alcohol

Element 7: Record the Compilation of the Total Effects of Consuming Alcohol versus Current Values

Combined Perceived Benefits of Ceasing Alcohol	Aligned to Values?	Combined Perceived Benefits of Alcohol	Aligned to Values?

Element 8: Record and Replace the Fears That Are Holding You Back

Current Fears Based on Old Beliefs	New Positive Beliefs and Benefits That Replace Them

Element 9: Record Your Current Actions Involving Alcohol and Replace Them with New Actions

Current Actions I Need to Change	New Replacement Actions That Will Assist Me

Element 10: Prepare Answers to Likely Questions and Statements Regarding Your New Habit

Situations or Questions I May Need a Response To	Response Options

Element 11: Write Your Commitment Statement

My Commitment Statement

Element 12: Document and Reward Milestones

My Milestones	Date	Reached?	My Reward	Taken?
1 Day				
2 Day				
3 Day				
4 Day				
5 Day				
6 Day				
1 Week				
2 Weeks				
3 Weeks				
1 Month (30 Days)				
2 Months				
3 Months				
6 Months				
1 Year				
2 Years				
3 Years				

Element 13: Plan Your Start Date and *Start*

Festivities I Have Taken into Account	Start Date

Acknowledgments

Many individual relationships and events throughout my life have enabled me to have the psychological and spiritual awareness to write this book. As it is with all our lives, not all these seemed pleasant and helpful at the time, and it is only with greater enlightenment and hindsight that it becomes evident these were lessons we needed to learn for our soul's greater good.

With this in mind, I would like to acknowledge all the people I have connected with in the past for the influence or effect they have had on my learning journey. Some have been very happy to have known me, and some would have rather we never crossed paths, though each and every one of you was necessary for making me who I am today, and for that I sincerely thank you. I hope that the message in this book is able to assist you or someone you care about in a positive way.

I wish to acknowledge and thank both Bob Proctor (Matrixx coaching event) and Brendon Burchard (Experts Academy coaching event and Total Product Blueprint program) for the expert information, motivation, and inspiration that helped me believe I could put my years of experience into a book and a program to assist others. Without their expert information and coaching this book would not exist.

I would like to thank my friend Shane, who was kind enough to read through the four hundred pages of my original transcript (while on his vacation) and offer valuable insight from a separate perspective.

To my editor Amanda at Amanda Rooker Editing, I owe a huge debt of gratitude. She really embraced the message and intent of this book and worked passionately to help me reduce the content to an acceptable level. This was done in a way that was very sensitive to the nature of the book and my unique style of getting my story of struggle and solution across. She showed empathy and compassion when I revealed and discussed more of the personal side of my struggle with alcohol and committed enthusiasm in condensing and fine-tuning my message to make the reading experience as valuable as possible. I highly recommend her.

Rightfully so, my wife and sons deserve praiseworthy credit for loving and supporting me through thick and thin. At times, during the darkest days, I couldn't see this, as alcohol had filled those days with feelings of sadness, frustration, and quiet desperation. But Donna could see glimpses of what I thought was long lost: the real me, still shining through cracks in the darkness. The underlying love of my family was a driving force and catalyst for me to reach the tipping point of really committing to being alcohol-free. They continue to support me in my commitment to help as many other people as possible by sharing my journey and message. To Donna and my boys, I love you and thank you for being who you are.

Thank you to everyone at Morgan James Publishing who has supported my project so completely and has allowed me to share the Alcohemy program with a much wider audience than I ever could have otherwise.

And last, as written in the poem "Invictus," "I thank whatever gods may be; For my unconquerable soul." There is a spirit that resides within us all, and it is the reason we are alive. It gives us purpose and meaning. It's the drive to be the best we can, to create, to accomplish, to love, to live, and to experience. Alcohol serves only to diminish all these essential desires of life, and it was the power of my internal spirit that drove me to break free. I am eternally grateful to this power that reintroduced me to my true self and the true knowledge that I am the master of my fate and the captain of my soul.

About the Author

David Norman was an ordinary Aussie bloke who, like more than 400 million other people around the world, developed an alcohol dependency. He went from a young lad brimming with a passion for adventure and discovery to leading a life of struggle and quiet desperation because of chronic alcohol-related problems. In an determined effort to break these shackles, David dedicated himself to researching the mind, body, and spirit and developed a process of not only becoming permanently alcohol-free, but most importantly to him, doing it by himself in a completely private and discreet way with no public embarrassment. His mission is to share this Alcohemy process and help as many people as possible around the world in similar circumstances. David lives with his wife and two sons in Hervey Bay, Queensland, Australia.